GOD, CAN YOU LOVE ME?

GOD, CAN YOU LOVE ME?

even when
i can't
love you?

CHRYSTAL HANSEN

Author photo by Susan Rose Photography

DESTINY IMAGE® PUBLISHERS, INC.

P.O. Box 310, Shippensburg, PA 17257-0310

"Speaking to the Purposes of God for This Generation and for the Generations to Come."

This book and all other Destiny Image, Revival Press, MercyPlace, Fresh Bread, Destiny Image Fiction, and Treasure House books are available at Christian bookstores and distributors worldwide.

For a U.S. bookstore nearest you, call 1-800-722-6774.

For more information on foreign distributors, call 717-532-3040.

Reach us on the Internet: www.destinyimage.com.

ISBN 10: 0-7684-3216-2
ISBN 13: 978-0-7684-3216-9

For Worldwide Distribution, Printed in the U.S.A.

1 2 3 4 5 6 7 8 9 10 11 / 13 12 11 10

THIS BOOK IS LOVINGLY DEDICATED TO:

My mom and dad, Walt and Dolores Grieb.

I am forever grateful for your extraordinary care and love for me throughout my life Thanks, Daddy, for your amazing heart of love, nurture, and tenderness. I can never repay you and I will always be grateful. You showed the love of Christ through your fathering. And thanks Mom, you are the one who faithfully modeled and taught me utter dependency on the heavenly Father. Your example kept me tethered to Christ through my journey. Your loving prayers still ring in my heart today.

And to:

My beloved and supportive husband, Ken.

Though we would have chosen another path for our lives, God saw fit to walk us down this one. Honey, I couldn't have made it through this journey without you. For you have lived a life of character, integrity, and faithfulness being completely committed to the destiny of our lives. I love you more than ever.

CONTENTS

FOREWORD

In 1996, I WENT FOR THE FIRST TIME to minister at the church of my friend, Ken Hansen, who I had known since we were both in youth group together in Buffalo, New York. After the services, we went back to his home, where I would be staying for the weekend. I distinctly remember that evening, meeting Chrystal for the first time, when she was in the midst of the darkest days of her life—which you will read about in this book. She was withdrawn, noncommunicative, and I remember just sensing that she was in incredible despair.

To see Chrystal today, strong, confident, centered in Christ, and fully embracing her life and calling in God, is to see a miracle.

I have been a personal witness of the truth of which you are about to read in this amazing book. I have seen firsthand not only the miracle that God has worked in Chrystal's life, but the effect of powerful principles that she learned through this remarkable journey that she now shares with so many in the Body of Christ.

There is much that is available to us through the life and love of Christ, but so often, we do not access the fullness of the healing and restoration made available to us. Too often, our healing remains "potential," rather than something we walk in. In this book, Chrystal shares from the authority of her own testimony not only what God did for her, but proven, balanced, scriptural strategies of how God's Word can make a powerful difference for you.

On a regular basis, our ministry invites Chrystal and her ministry team to come and teach the principles in this book to our staff. We have all personally benefited from the anointing that rests on Chrystal's life to "heal the brokenhearted, and proclaim liberty to the captives."

Chrystal's message is powerful because it immediately brings a sense of purpose and hope to the hearer, but it also requires those who desire transformation and healing to walk out the reality of what it means to come into maturity in Christ. This is not an "instant fix" manual, but rather, a genuine pathway to transformation that can begin today, with tools that can be walked out for the journey of life.

The book you hold in your hand is the testimony of a life that has been dramatically and powerfully transformed, and it shares the keys that can bring that same change into your life, or the life of someone you love.

In His Grace,
Dr. Robert Stearns
Executive Director, Eagles Wings
New York

AN AMAZING ADVENTURE WITH GOD

IN THE SUMMER OF 1996, my husband, Ken, and I saw our world come crashing down around us as I was overtaken by severe depression and an inability to cope with the pressures of life and ministry. Together, we sought professional help from a psychiatrist and a psychologist, and I was eventually diagnosed with bipolar disorder. Though treated with numerous antidepressant medications, I continued to experience rapid high and low emotional cycles, along with alarming psychotic episodes. Ken and I continually sought God's healing for the unexplained pain lodged in my heart.

"To live again" became the cry of my heart. As I battled with mental illness, God surprised me and gave me so much more than my life back. He miraculously restored my mind and brought healing to my wounded and broken heart. I pray that sharing my journey back from severe mental illness will offer a message of hope for the hurting and the desperate. And to the many friends and family members who walk alongside of those suffering, be assured and filled with hope that God still performs miracles today.

Have you ever felt frustrated or overwhelmed? Have you ever lost the will to go on? Reading about my journey will inspire and encourage you to move forward, one day at a time. God has given me a passion to help others experience the miraculous transforming power of Christ.

Over the past decade, I have been focused on developing teachings and curriculums for small groups, helping individuals journey through their inner struggles of brokenness and shattered dreams into a thriving relationship with Christ. It is a process and a lifelong journey in God, but when you sense His healing hand and restorative power in your heart, you will find that the journey is an amazing adventure with God.

Only You

There's a fog all around
There's a dew on the ground
There's a coldness in the air
Filled with anguish and despair

I have nowhere to run
I have nowhere to hide
I have no one left to see
my desperation inside

I need the Light of the world
I need the dawn of a new day

I need the opening of a door
I need the path of a new way

It's all in You
It's all up to You

Take me on a journey to find myself
To find who I was meant to be
To find who You designed me to be

Take me on a journey;
To the core of my being
To the depths of my soul
To the innermost places of my heart

Only You know what will be found and discovered
Only You know what will be overturned and made new
Only You know, Only You

Only You can open the recesses of my soul
Only You can navigate the path
Only You can excavate the soil of my heart
Only You can, Only You

Take me on a journey
Take me to find You
Take me on a journey
To find Only You.

—Chrystal Hansen, 2005

Chapter 1

To Live Again

"DADDY, COME HOME QUICK," the young voice pleaded on the other end of the phone. "Mommy is sick!"

My husband, Ken, rushed home to find me curled up in the fetal position, sobbing hysterically in the middle of the kitchen floor. Our children were encircled around me, almost as if to protect their mommy until daddy could get there and take over. Our seven-year-old son was praying for me; our five-year-old daughter was stroking my hair and telling me everything was going to be alright; while our two-year-old looked on with eyes the size of saucers. Unable to gain control of my flood of emotions, all I could do was cry out, "I just want to live again!"

The full mental breakdown that I experienced in the summer of 1996 could be compared to when your computer locks up and although you keep typing in the data, the computer won't read it. You wonder what has gone wrong and why the information you're entering isn't being processed the way it's supposed to be. No matter what you do, you can't figure out where the connection broke or how to fix the problem. Then a frustrating message begins flashing across the screen: "Error... cannot compute."

I had always tried to be very in control, able to accomplish whatever goals I set out to achieve. When the dam broke that day in the middle of my kitchen floor, I could no longer figure out what I needed to do to get through the day. Things went from bad to worse as I began to experience severe anxiety attacks. Overwhelming waves of panic and fear literally froze me in that moment in time. Those powerful emotions would paralyze me. After the emotions played themselves out, my rational mind would return, just enough to get me through the anxiety attack.

For a period of time, up to 2½ hours, I would be trapped in a vicious circle of unrestrained panic until the cycle played itself out. I didn't know what might trigger an attack or how to shut it off once it started. If I was at church and I started hyperventilating and crying, friends or staff would take me to a back room where my emotions could play themselves out. I remember feeling like a spectator, watching as one part of me tried to focus on what was happening, while the other half of my brain fought against the wave of panic. The other part of me seemed to realize I had absolutely no control over what was happening and just gave up as the tidal wave of emotions totally engulfed me.

I never knew when one of these attacks would happen. I lived in fear of embarrassing my husband in public or of not being able to take care of my three small children. What if this happened when I was driving the car or in the grocery store? These waves of panic started to come more and more frequently, and I began to slip farther and farther away from any kind of normality.

Brain Shutdown

Like many people, I had a daily routine. As my condition worsened, I found I was unable to perform even the simplest everyday tasks. My mind gradually shut down and I no longer knew what I should do first. Without being able to initiate certain sequences, routine tasks, like brushing my teeth, became impossible to complete. I would pick up my toothbrush and stand at the sink for an hour, trying to figure out what to do next. Although I had done that task thousands of times before, I could not process my thoughts into actions.

On one occasion, when I wanted to fix lunch for my kids, I pulled out a box of macaroni and reached for the pan. I looked back and forth between the two items I held in my hands. I knew I'd made it before, but I couldn't pull from my memory banks the actual steps I needed to take in order to accomplish it. I could not remember what to do first. Should I put water in the pan or dump the contents of the box in first? Struggling to do this simple task triggered an anxiety attack. This task was not new to me. Why couldn't I access the information needed to do this simple task?

When it got so bad that I could not remember how to dress myself, I knew I was in big trouble. I was already on medication and working through some of the issues that had surfaced in previous counseling sessions. I could no longer access the information I needed to function in life. I could see events happening all around me but could not clear the fog in my brain enough to participate.

(I have been told by friends and family that during that period I spent a lot of time staring off into space.)

I would awaken in the morning, sit on the edge of the bed, look at myself in the mirror, and wonder what I was supposed to do next.

No logical progression of thoughts would come. My husband would be there to get the kids off to school. He helped me get dressed, fixed my breakfast, and told me to lie on the couch until he came home at lunch time. Friends showed up during the day to check on me, knowing I couldn't care for myself.

"Detachments of reality" began. People would be talking to me, I could see their lips moving, but I could not understand what they were saying. This triggered more anxiety attacks. I became even more afraid to talk to people. Living any kind of normal life seemed to be slipping farther and farther out of my reach, with no apparent way to stop this journey to nowhere.

I have since learned that this condition is what professionals refer to as Depersonalization Disorder. It is characterized by a feeling of detachment from, or being an outside observer of, one's mental processes or body. The sensation is like being in a dream. The phenomenon causes distress or impairs work, social, or personal functioning.[1]

At the time all I knew was the struggle to stay alive. I was on every antidepressant drug available from Lithium to Effexor. My doctors tried every combination imaginable to find something to get me to function normally. Nothing worked for any length of time. At one point they recommended hospitalization, but my husband was afraid that if I went in, I might never come out. He did everything he could to keep me safe, while he continued to pastor our church and care for our children.

Support of the Church

It came to the point where the doctors told my husband that I had to completely drop all of my responsibilities at the church for several months or be admitted to the hospital. We were told that I was in no condition to function as a pastor's wife and that it was adding stress to my already fragile mental stability. I sadly watched as everything I had worked to achieve all my life slipped out of my hands. I could no longer function normally as a wife and mother, and now my ability to serve God was slipping away as well.

My husband got up before our congregation the first Sunday that I was gone and gave them some very basic information as to why I was not there. He explained that I was struggling with what we thought was clinical depression and that, per doctor's orders, I needed three months off to rest. He asked them not to call but encouraged them to send cards and especially to pray for our family as we walked this out. We were very surprised at the support we received from every parishioner in the church. One by one they assured my husband they would pray for us. I cried when Ken shared their response, "Tell her to take as much time as she needs. We just want her to get well."

On good days, I would try to be as "normal" as possible and do things like go to the grocery store. But if I saw somebody from the church I would panic, thinking I would have to explain why I was well enough to get groceries but not able to attend church on Sunday. Instead of disapproval, they always gave me an encouraging smile and a gentle hello. One dear elderly couple from the church met me in the grocery aisle one day. As I came toward them they gave me a very simple greeting, then lovingly smiled and said, "We love you, and we want you to get well. So hurry back, but take your time." It was those kinds of comments and the love of all these dear people that actually aided in the process of wholeness for me.

In his second letter to the Corinthians, Paul talks about how the support of the church strengthened him during the many trials he faced on his various missionary journeys (see 2 Cor. 8:1-7). I too came to realize that the support of the local body of believers has to strengthen the ministers, just as much as the ministers are to strengthen the Body. As we learned more about my illness, we let our loving congregation know what my progress was and asked for their continued prayers and support. I held onto their love and kindness when nothing else in my life made any sense.

A New Year—A New Diagnosis

From August 1996 to January 1997, my treatment was primarily focused on clinical depression. I was prescribed close to 1600 milligrams of drugs per day to get me to a minimal functioning level. I was receiving counseling and was being coached by a spiritual mentor. With all of this therapy, I honestly thought that within a few months of rest I'd be able to put it all behind me and move back into a normal lifestyle.

As we approached the end of the prescribed three-month rest period, I realized that I was in no condition to go back to work or handle normal household responsibilities. I was still experiencing a deep inner sadness, which was now joined with a sense that I was not getting any better. There seemed to be no cure in sight from the daily regimen of medication. I had been looking forward to the New Year, thinking I would be able to resume some of my everyday activities. However, as January 1997 approached, I realized that this was a much bigger problem than I had perceived.

On January 2, 1997, I received some news that pushed me over the edge. I received a phone call telling me that my grandfather had passed away. I was dumbfounded. I knew he had been ill, but my first thought was, *Lord, why now?* I was angry at God for taking my grandfather from me when I was already sad and depressed. As I cried out to the Lord, I literally heard Him say, "My timing is perfect."

(Later, I would come to understand that my depression and sadness were connected to the loss of my father. So when my grandfather died, it opened up that unresolved wound in my heart, the root of all my personal struggles.)

At the time, however, I didn't understand. I thought God was incredibly cruel to add this loss of a loved one to an already overwhelming time in my life. I didn't realize that I hadn't yet reached the bottom of the pit where God would be my only refuge. I just knew I was hurting, and nobody seemed to be able to do anything to relieve the pain.

My Life Is a Ghost Town

As a matter of fact, I was quite angry with the Lord for not healing me. After all, I had given my life in service to Him. I had done everything I thought I was supposed to do as a Christian and yet I was still suffering and was incapacitated by this horrible illness. What kind of God would be so cruel and unappreciative of my efforts to please Him? I'd been taught that He was supposed to be my joy and my strength. Why was I not seeing either in my life when others were attaining that joy? As these questions swirled in my brain, I began to experience a severe crisis of faith. Where was God in all this? Did He even exist, or had I believed a lie all my life? Even if there was a God, did I want to serve someone so cruel and uncaring?

I looked at my life and saw that I couldn't function as a wife or a mother. I could no longer serve as a minister or even pray for the hurting in our congregation. I couldn't dress myself or do any of the things that a normal person should be able to do. My emotions threw me into such a depressed state of mind that I ended up wondering, *Why live? What is the point?* The only conclusion I seemed to be able to come to was that I was totally useless to my family, my church, and my God.

It got to the point where people from the church would do my laundry and get my children dressed and take them to church on Sunday. I know they were all trying to help, but it was demoralizing to me because those were things I was supposed to be doing. I felt like I was a burden to my husband and an unfit mother to my children. There was also the guilt of not being able to serve side-by-side with my husband in ministry. I felt as if they would all be better off without me. That's how suicidal thinking starts, and I was well on the road to seriously considering that as an option.

This was my state of mind when the news came about the death of my grandfather. I hung up the phone and felt like screaming. I couldn't take it anymore. I clamped my mouth closed, ran to my little prayer room, sat at the desk, and wrote frantically in my journal to try to relieve the pressure and anger building in my brain.

Oh God, where do I find the words to describe my state of existence? No words can express the agony my entire being is experiencing. "Clinical Depression," that's the medical term given to my state; yet that doesn't begin to touch the devastation, hopelessness, and despair that has taken over my life. In every avenue of life, the sign "street closed" is displayed.

It's as if I am looking at an old western ghost town. The tumbleweed is tossing here and there; the dirt and debris is swirling around; and the broken shutters of old wooden buildings are creaking and crashing against each other. The finishing touch to this scene is the haunting sound of the wind whistling, howling, and exuding the unfathomable realization that life no longer exists here.

As I gaze upon this scene, I am not frightened, nor unnerved. Ironically I feel a kinship, an understanding with this little town. For it depicts the barrenness of my own soul and whispers the non-existence of my own life. "The non-existence of life…" Can that describe my state of existence?

Scripture is full of paradoxes: to lead, you serve; to be first is to be last; to be glorified with Christ is to first suffer with Christ; to be strong, you become weak; and to live you must die. Yes, the "non-existence of life" describes my state.

My energy drained, I cried out, "Oh God, where are You, and what are You doing? I can't do this anymore; I'm finished. I'm done." In that moment, I lost all physical strength, and my head just dropped and hit the desk. I didn't have the physical strength to lift my head or even to call for help. In utter despair, I flatly declared, "Lord, I don't want to live anymore. I'm not going to take my life, but I think You need to take it." Utterly devoid of emotion, I said, "You know what, Lord? I'm done. This is it."

I closed my eyes hoping I would go to sleep and never wake up. I saw myself just lying down as if I was being laid out in a casket. I said, "Yes, Lord, that's me. There's just no life left in me. I'm dead; I'm done." Then I saw a white, cloudy thing swirling around my face, and the Lord said, "That's My breath; your whole life is in Me." Still feeling like there wasn't any life left in me, I said, "Just take Your breath from me, Lord. If I cannot function, if I cannot regain my life, I don't want to live at all."

When my husband found me, I looked at him and said, "I think I'm just going to take all of the medicine and go to sleep and never wake up." To his shocked expression I just said, "What's so shocking? It's my life, and there's nothing worthwhile left in me." Severely shaken, my husband immediately called the doctors and the people who were supporting of us.

They talked me out of that dangerous line of thinking and made me agree to call one of them before acting on any type of self-destructive thoughts. Just knowing these people knew that I was wrestling with those kinds of thoughts made me feel they would be there for me. Somehow, that prevented me from keeping those thoughts silent or taking any self-destructive action because of them.

I now understand how suicide can look like a viable alternative when one is at the bottom of the pit of depression. I never walked that path, but unfortunately, many depressed people do.

Can You Still Love Me?

At least I felt like God heard me that night in prayer when I told Him I didn't want to live like that anymore. The vision I saw of myself helped me to understand that if the breath of God was going to do anything in my life, it was going to be all God and not me. I had always tried to be what I thought God wanted me to be and what people needed me to be. When all of that was taken away, all of my strength was gone, too. It was from that time on that God began to bring strength to me, one step at a time.

A major realization came shortly after my ghost town vision. I was lying on the couch utterly frustrated with myself, unable to concentrate enough to read my Bible. I said to the Lord, "I can't read Your Word anymore. I can't pray the way I'm used to praying, the way I've been taught. I don't really want to worship; I can't go to church and

I can't handle being with people." Totally discouraged by my lack of progress, I cried out, "Lord, I hope You can love me, when I can't love You in return."

There were moments during my illness were I had great clarity when it came to conversing with God. Looking back on this, I am amazed at His divine intervention into my state of mind. And I am overcome with His love and mercy through which he spoke so clearly, to enable me to take the necessary steps toward wholeness.

That comment really showed the state of my belief system at the time. I believed that if I couldn't be the Christian that I thought I needed to be for God, then He wouldn't love me.

The Lord spoke very strongly to me at that moment, asking me, "What do you do when your children are sick?"

"I put them on the couch, keep them warm, give them their medicine, and make sure they're comfortable," I answered, as if I was in a face-to-face conversation with Him.

He asked me, "Do you want to play with them? Do you want them to get off the couch and run outside or do their chores when they're sick and have a fever?"

"Of course not," I responded. "I don't really want them to talk. I want them to rest and be quiet."

He said, "Bingo, that's where you are. You're sick, and I'm going to take care of you. Lie there and be quiet. I'm not expecting anything from you. I will bring you what you need."

The Lord wanted me to receive His care and covering because I was in need of healing. I had a choice as to whether I would willingly stay under this shelter and covering and allow Him to do what needed to be done. It may seem like a "no-brainer," but after being driven by works all my life, it was not easy to allow the Lord to lay a covering over me and to just rest and heal. I had to release my old mind-set and allow myself to receive something for which I did not work.

That was the day my performance issues began to die, and I began to realize that God loved me, even when I couldn't love Him. Like many other believers, I had always said God's love was unconditional, but deep inside I figured that still meant I had to do something or else God wouldn't be able to love me. God totally kicked that crutch out from under me. I was at a place where I couldn't do anything for Him or for anyone else. He told me He still loved me and wanted to give me the help that I needed. What an amazing revelation! It would forever change my relationship with the Lord.

Later, I discovered what David had written in Psalm 18:4-6 and found that it described my state of mind very accurately. Obviously, David had experienced times of severe distress in his life as well.

> The cords of death entangled me; the torrents of destruction over-whelmed me. The cords of the grave coiled around me; the snares of death confronted me. In my distress I called to the Lord; I cried to my God for help. From His temple He heard my voice; my cry came before Him, into His ears (Psalm 18:4-6).

While grieving over my grandfather, I experienced a feeling of death come over me. I felt like there was positively no way out of my situation other than by the direct intervention of God. My Christianity hadn't gotten me out. Worship hadn't gotten me out. Bible reading and devotions hadn't gotten me out. I felt totally surrounded on every side, and knew the only way out was for God to hear my cry.

I know that God did hear my cry for help, and He answered me by assuring me that He would bring me the help I needed. He did indeed give me what I needed, but it was not the way I wanted.

Lancing the Wound

I went to my grandfather's funeral. I stood at a distance looking at him, having a very difficult time keeping my composure. My mother whispered into my ear, "This is where your father was laid out and buried." I let out an internal scream and said to myself, "Oh my God, I have been here before." In that moment, God lanced something deep in my heart and opened up a wound that had never healed—a wound that had been festering for years because none of us knew it was even there. Somehow I made it through the funeral, but I knew I needed to talk through what I had felt standing there.

I went into intensive counseling, trying to discover why I felt that I had been in that funeral home before. The counselors helped me to begin to understand how the grief that was in my heart resulted from what my mother went through right before I was born. All the grief, all the sadness, and all the despair my mother experienced standing next to the casket of her husband of only 11 months was transferred to the child she carried in her womb. Through no conscious effort on my mother's part, the grief she was experiencing lodged in my spirit as well.

Studies have found that good, peaceful things can be lodged into the spirit of a baby from playing soothing music and reading them comforting books. This is true even while the child is still in the womb. It stands to reason then that something in the mother's life as painful as the death of a spouse could also get lodged in an unborn child's spirit.[2] God used the death of my grandfather to get me in touch with this deeply buried grief.

When God lanced that wound, all that had been buried in my heart and spirit came out full blast. My depression began to make sense as we worked through the grief and pain I had carried for my father all those years. However, it also triggered bouts of extremely accelerated thinking and a lot of hyperactivity. Days of deep depression followed, where I slept the majority of the time. This back-and-forth behavior was finally diagnosed as bipolar disorder.

Bipolar Is My Diagnosis

Bipolar disorder used to be called manic-depressive disorder. Bipolar basically means having two poles: your high and your low. Someone who is diagnosed as bipolar has emotional swings that go from extremely high to extremely low, with an inability to regulate them.[3] In my case, my moods could change in a day, even cycle around several times a day—which is referred to as a rapid cycle specifier.

We began to see that I had already been experiencing what is known as seasonal cycling. During the first part of the year and into the spring, I would experience depression. It seemed that when summer hit and I could get outside, I would gradually come out of that season of depression. As a matter of fact, once I began to understand and read about the characteristics of what a person who is bipolar exhibits, I realized that I had gone through almost all of them. I think the only exception was that I did not go out and spend large sums of money. Many people diagnosed with bipolar disease go on shopping sprees to try to alleviate the pain, sometimes spending thousands of dollars. I'm sure my husband was thankful that I didn't exhibit that symptom.

I also began experiencing brief psychotic episodes (also known as brief reactive psychosis), which is a short-term break from reality.[4] I would struggle with whether or not what I saw and heard was real. I could be sitting right next to someone but not be sure if they were real or not. Not being able to determine what is real and what isn't is a very real component of bipolar behavior. Part of the process I had to go through to deal with these brief psychotic episodes was to ask questions of those I trusted who would help me sort between the real and the unreal.

At first, I was relieved that we finally knew what the root cause of all this was. I could identify myself as bipolar, and it gave definition to what never had meaning in my life before. I understood what I had wrestled with all my life, and it began to make sense. But as I stayed in intense counseling for one year, then two years, and then three years, it wore on me. I realized I couldn't be normal and be bipolar. How could this have happened to me, and what did it mean to my future? To find the answers I needed, I had to go back to the months before I was born. This search would eventually lead me to the place where God could not only heal me but help me to truly live again.

As I take you on my journey from mental illness to wholeness, I want you to benefit from what I learned along the way. Therefore, at the end of each chapter I have provided a place for you to journal your amazing adventure that God has you on: "My Adventure and Journey With God." Your journey will be different than mine and it may not seem like an adventure yet, but trust me, God is looking forward to showing you His amazing love. Please take the time to read through, journal, and do the exercises suggested before moving on to the next chapter. You will not only gain more insight and understanding about what I walked through, but it will help you deal with your life circumstances or hidden hurt in your own life. I pray that as you read my journey, it will make your own journey easier because of the insights you gained.

My Adventure and Journey With God

1. Have you ever honestly wrestled with the thought, *Can God still love me, when I can't serve or do things for Him?* Journal how this may be impacting your view of God.

2. In your lonely places, how has God spoken to you? Read and reflect on Psalm 55:1-8,16-17.

3. Journal any deep, hidden pain that you have sensed. Take comfort in the fact that the Psalms contain not only praises and thanksgiving but also reflections of brokenness. Read and meditate upon Psalm 42:4-5.

4. Have you ever had to deal with the unexpected death of a loved one? Briefly explain how you dealt with your grief and pain.

a. How did this death of a loved one affect your relationship with God? Or how did it affect your relationship with other loved ones?

b. Were you confused or angry with God about this death? Have you ever honestly shared your feelings with God? If not, take the time to do so right now. Be honest in telling God your feelings. Remember that the Psalms record deep feelings of confusion, anger, and despair. Read Psalm 61:2; 94:18-19.

5. Pray and ask God to give you further insights into areas that He may desire to reveal in you and bring healing in your life. Here is a sample prayer to help you get started:

Heavenly Father, I desire for You to do a deep work in my heart and life. And I know it begins with acknowledging my need of You in the areas of my heart that I don't understand, that are filled with pain and hurt and that are in need of comfort. I ask You to be with me in these places, comfort my broken heart, bring Your truth to set me free and Your joy to take the place of my despair. And through Your great love and mercy may my life bring forth Your glory and testify of Your great love (see Isaiah 61:2-3,6).

I also recommend that you re-read my poem, "Only You," at the end of the Introduction and use that as a personal prayer for your time with God.

CHAPTER 2

A Bittersweet Beginning

As we searched for the root cause of my battle with depression and then the onset of bipolar symptoms, the time just prior to my birth always surfaced. My biological father, Carl, was a traveling evangelist who had experienced many miracles and healings in his ministry. God had used him in mighty ways all throughout his ministry. He had even experienced a gradual physical healing in his own body from a spinal injury he received when he was hit by a car at the age of four. The doctors had done what they could but felt the damage would eventually result in a curvature of the spine that could leave him confined to a wheelchair by the time he was 21.

Carl had to quit school at the age of 15 after being diagnosed with ulcerative colitis. The doctors had no real protocol on how to treat him and essentially gave up, telling my grandparents there was nothing more that medicine could do for him. Out of desperation, my grandmother took Carl to Kathryn Kuhlman miracle services held every Friday in Pittsburgh. In one service, Miss Kuhlman announced from the platform that a young man was being healed of a curvature in his spine. Carl went forward, and she prayed for him. Over the next month a gradual straightening of the spine occurred until all signs of the curvature were gone.

When my parents married, Carl had already been battling and living with colitis for about 10 years. My father believed and professed wholeheartedly that a miracle of healing would be seen in his physical body. He was so convinced that God would supernaturally heal him that he walked with confident faith, believing, in spite of the physical condition.

My mom and Carl were married only 11 months when the Lord decided to take Carl to Heaven. This left my family exhausted and broken, for they too had hoped and believed that God would do a miracle and heal him. When no miracle came and my father died just days before his twenty-sixth birthday, grief entered into the hearts of all the family members, including me as his unborn child.

I was born six weeks later on Mother's Day weekend, just one week after their first anniversary would have been. My mother was now 24 years old, a widow, and a single parent.

Tell Me About My Dad

My mother told me that my father had talked and prayed over me constantly, which formed a connection between us. When my father was taken, hurt and pain entered my spirit. Somehow I also sensed that even though I was the granddaughter, the daughter, and the niece, I was all that was left of the son, the husband, and the brother to my grieving family. The family saw Carl's life continue through the blessing of my life.

I longed to know more about the father I had never met. I wanted to know how was I like him and if I had mannerisms like his. I couldn't get answers firsthand because he was no longer a part of my life. I could study pictures of him, but I would never have that special father/daughter relationship with him that I saw the other kids having. Even at a very young age, I felt a sense of loss that I couldn't explain. I had no real conscious memory of my father yet the feeling of missing him was very real.

I could not understand, let alone explain to the people around me, how I could miss someone I had never known. I had a lot of questions and I couldn't express what I was feeling inside. The adults who raised me never suspected this sense of loss, and I could not have realized how the depth of the grief I was experiencing would affect me.

Connected in the Womb

We have since learned that there is a spirit connection formed when a child is still in the womb. We know from studies that a child knows his mother's voice and responds to the peace or anxiousness of the mother. Studies in both the psychological and scientific realm now encourage both parents to interact with a child in the womb by playing soothing music as well as talking and reading to the unborn baby. Experts say that the baby is receiving those good things from its parents and that there is a definite connection happening between them even while the child is still in the womb.

Not long ago we thought it was impossible for prenates to have any truly personal or significant experiences. We didn't see that they could have a working mind. In retrospect, our false beliefs about their brain power obscured the fact that babies in the uterine world were indeed having potentially rich experiences, establishing patterns of interaction, listening to music and conversation, and as tests ultimately proved, were committing them to memory. Numerous experiments have made it clear that prenates who have the opportunity to hear stories and music repeated to them in utero can demonstrate recognition for this material later in life. Prenates memorize the voices of their mothers and fathers in utero. Spectrographic analysis of voice and cry sounds as early as 26 weeks of gestation show how far babies of this age have already progressed in adopting the voice characteristics of the mother. In other research, babies have demonstrated immediately after birth a preference for their mother's voice and their native language. The womb turns out to be a stimulating place and is, in many ways, a school. These studies have proven: (1) that babies in the womb are alert, aware, and attentive to activities involving voice, touch, and music; (2) that babies benefit from these activities by forming stronger relationships with their parents and their parents with them.[1]

It stands to reason that if good things—such as a sense of security, trust, and love—from both mom and dad can be experienced in the womb, the reverse is likely also true. When something goes wrong and trauma enters the life of a mother, then that is also transmitted into an infant's spirit.

I was told that my father often laid hands on my mother's stomach and prayed and talked to me. We now know that those things cause a very real connection between the unborn child and that parent. I think that I did hear his voice and somehow understood that there was this person on the outside praying for and wanting me to be born. When I came into that physical environment, I instinctively looked for that person, but he was gone. I believe I experienced the sadness and grief associated with losing a loved one even before I was born.

> I have known Chrystal for ten years and have witnessed an emotional state of sadness in her whenever Mother's Day and her birthday came around. We discovered there was sadness and grief attached to the death of her father. I observed several ministry sessions where Chrystal was able to feel what the little girl and even the baby in the womb felt when she stopped hearing her father's voice. I observed a longing to know her birth father and a searching for why she felt the way she felt. She had mental pictures and a sense of being in the womb and not wanting to uncurl and a sense that "why should I live now that he is gone." She said she felt the presence of the Lord and perceived Him comforting her.[2]

It's important to realize that unborn children recognize both positive and negative things in their spirit, though they may not be able to process those feelings in a comprehensive way until they are older.

> During pregnancy, the parent's perception of the environment is chemically communicated to the fetus through the placenta, the cellular barrier between the maternal and fetal blood. The mother's blood-borne emotional chemicals cross the placenta and affect the same target cells in the fetus as those in the parent. Though the developing child is "unaware" of the details (i.e., the stories) evoking the mother's emotional response, they are aware of the emotion's physiological consequences and sensations.[3]

My First Five Years

For the first five years of my life, my mother raised me with the help of my father's parents. I was surrounded by a family who loved and cared for me. My mom taught and modeled for me a dependency on God that I have never forgotten and I believe influenced me greatly. I remember countless times hearing her pray: in the car, at home, and during church. She also sang many wonderful old hymns and songs that I still love today. Because of her strong influence early in my life, my heart clung to my heavenly Father through all my later pain and confusion.

My mother had to work full time during those first few years, so I spent most of my days with my grandmother. My time with her is a very positive and good memory. My grandmother was always praying, singing, and depending on God. I love the verse in Second Timothy 1:5, where Paul refers to the fact that Timothy's mother and grandmother had taught him the Scriptures from childhood and imparted faith to him as he grew up. I believe that both my mother and grandmother imparted much faith and prayer into my life. I know my life as a believer is as grounded and rooted as it is because of the faith and prayer these women imparted to my life.

Most of my memories during those first five years are of my grandparents' house. They had 2½ acres of land filled with apple, pear, and cherry trees, berry bushes, and grapevines, as well as a huge vegetable garden. We were always outside in the yard gardening, walking the property, or climbing the fruit trees. I used to help plant the garden as well as the flowers that lined the front of the house and the walkway to the mailbox. My grandparents were gardeners, and my grandmother canned everything they grew. I would help her can the tomatoes, jellies, applesauce, peaches, plus anything else we grew in the garden that year.

One of my favorite memories was baking with my grandmother. She would take the leftover dough from the pies and make "sneaky-weezers," better known today as elephant ears. Where she got that name, I will never know, but how I loved those sugar and cinnamon covered "sneaky-weezers." My grandparents' land had several beautiful weeping willow trees, one of which was close to the house by the grapevines. We would eat under that tree every chance we got and then pick the grapes (when they were ripe) for our dessert.

My grandparents would mow a path through a wooded area where they would walk and pray. I remember accompanying my grandmother on many of those walks, where she would pray and talk to me about the Lord. She told me that my father Carl had walked and prayed that path on many occasions. I remember even as a little girl the connection it gave me with the man who had given me life. I would envision him walking and praying in that very place.

My grandparents also told me about the miracles and healings God did through Carl as he traveled with my aunt Judi. I remember one story about the time when they ran out of gas on their way to a meeting. Not wanting to be delayed, Carl placed a handkerchief in the opening of the gas tank, prayed, and believed that God would get them to their destination. Carl was right; God did.

My grandmother also told me how Carl would see angels, which challenged my young mind to believe in a real miracle-working God. I have carried that challenge to this day. The miracle I received was the fruit of those tiny seeds of faith planted in me during those wonderful conversations walking with my grandparents on their prayer path. Carl's picture hung on the wall in the living room of my grandparents' home, and I remember gazing into that picture, knowing that was my father. That picture is still vividly etched in my mind along with the wonderful stories my grandparents willingly shared with me.

My Dream

I had a dream when I was about four years old that I have carried with me all my life. In this dream I was at my grandparents' home standing in front of their porch with my mom, my aunt, and my grandparents. As I glanced down the sidewalk that led to the street, I saw a man standing under the huge willow tree that grew there. Instantly I knew it was Carl and I ran toward him. He picked me up and hugged me. Without saying a word, I knew he loved me, and without seeing his face, I knew it was my father. This dream brought comfort when I was young. It still brings a smile to my face and tears to my eyes. Our awesome God knows when we need a visual, a dream.

Aunt Judi Remembers Chrystal's Early Years

When Chrystal was about three years old, I moved to Pennsylvania and got to know my young niece a little better. My mother would babysit for Chrystal while her mother worked. My parents adored her and were so pleased that they could help and be an active part in Chrystal's formative years. Chrystal struck me as an assertive little girl, not afraid to voice her opinions, and she showed evidence of leadership even as a little girl. It was nothing for her to lead her little friends in whatever games they chose to play. At the time I had a German Shepherd dog named Heidi that Chrystal loved. She would watch *Lassie* on TV, then pretend she was Timmy and Heidi was Lassie.

I recall one incident when she was about four years old. We were washing Heidi in the basement, using some big stationary tubs, with Heidi's front legs in one tub and her back legs in the other tub. Chrystal stood up on an old wooden chair we had pulled up next to the sink as we were rubbing the soap suds all over the dog's back. Several times Chrystal stopped and looked out the window above the tubs, to the sky outside. There were big fluffy clouds drifting by and Chrystal would pause, staring at them intently, then say, "My daddy's up there." She seemed almost preoccupied with the idea, and I couldn't help but wonder what she thought about her daddy being in Heaven. This occurred two or three times during that "dog wash." She also seemed intent on "taking care of Mommy" during that same period of her life.[4]

Mom said I was a good baby and grew rapidly those first five years. After three years, my mother had enough income to move us into our own little apartment. I still spent days with my grandmother, but now we had a place of our own. Mom had fixed a room in the apartment for me as a play room. I remember I had an entire little kitchen set that I would play house with. My mother's father had given me a doll I named Susie. I loved Susie; she was practically as big as me. And I had many wonderful times with her in my play room pretending to cook and eat with her. Within those first five years of my life, my mother lost her mother to cancer and her father died of a heart attack. More grief, sorrow, and death entered our family.

I vaguely remember those events, nevertheless; studies show that these prenatal and early childhood memories definitely affect our attitudes toward life. Later in life I would learn that these conscious and unconscious memories left me with a fear of losing other loved ones, including my husband and my children. Such deep inner fear began to create trust issues that affected every major relationship in my life, even my relationship with God.

Memories of early trauma are there, underneath the surface. They're there in our dreams, attitudes, even in our vocabulary. People unconsciously walk around in them all day but are not aware of where they come from. These memories echo or ripple through our everyday experience. Early memories are like pebbles thrown into the water. The experience creates ripples that continue and expand, affecting people's lives profoundly. Psychologist Eric Erikson, in his Child Development Scale, uses trust or mistrust as the first building block of personality. The one which is chosen is the result of our first learned experience and that first experience is in the womb, during birth, or in that very critical period immediately after birth. Early messages create lifelong patterns of trust or distrust.[5]

All of our relationships in life are based on trust. I have heard it said, "Love is given, but trust is earned." Children who have had their trust violated, no matter how it happened, find it difficult to trust others (and even God) when they become adults.

My Adventure and Journey With God

Numerous external forces may shape us, but the family and its environment we have grown up in is the primary and most powerful influence that shapes our lives. It takes courage on our part to honestly look at our families of origin. We need to have the right attitude in doing so. It is not one of blame but of recognition that areas of my life may still be hurting from what I experienced as a young child. God is able to meet us when we come with open hearts to Him. He doesn't want the pain of unresolved memories to linger any longer in your heart, He came to heal broken hearts (see Isaiah 61). Will you let Him comfort and heal yours?

1. What memories, feelings, or attitudes do you have of the first five years of your life? Are they pleasant or are they sad? Think of the earliest memories you have of Mom and Dad, and write them here.

2. How would you describe the atmosphere in your home growing up?

3. Did you have much interaction with your grandparents and other relatives? Describe those relationships briefly.

4. Have you ever studied your family history? What have you discovered about your family tree? If you have never traced your family's roots, you may want to take the time to do so.

5. If you realize you are carrying hurts and pains from early childhood, seek counsel from your pastor or spiritual advisor first, then offer these painful places to God, asking Him to meet you in the pain and bring His comfort and healing to that part of your heart. Here is a sample prayer you may want to say:

Heavenly Father, I bring these painful places and memories (name each one) to You. Your word says that You came to heal my broken heart and comfort me. I am in need of both comfort and healing. I am tired of the pain and hurt so please come and bring Your strength and joy to fill these places (see Psalm 34:18).

6. Take time to write down any questions or concerns you may have, as well as any insights the Lord may give you. You may not understand their relevance at this time, but God may have you come back to them later on.

7. Even when we may not have had the family environment we may have desired, there are usually things we can thank the Lord for. Do so here. And if you have realized you had a very positive and nurturing environment early in life, take time to thank the Father also.

CHAPTER 3

THE BLESSING OF A DADDY

WHILE WORKING AT HORNE'S Department store in Pittsburgh, Pennsylvania, my mother met a man named Walt, who was remodeling the store. From my earliest recollection I prayed every night for a new daddy. I made prayer requests at Sunday school. So you would think that I would have been overjoyed when Walt started dating my mom. However, I remember thinking, *What is he doing here?* It was a strange feeling having someone else in my life.

I remember being shy and hiding from Walt. He would play along with the hiding game, and every time I would peek out from behind a chair or the couch, he would laugh and smile at me and say something funny. He was a kind and gentle man, never forcing a friendship, extending an invitation to know him, waiting for me to feel comfortable around him.

As they prepared for marriage, Walt gave me an engagement ring just like my mom. I wore that ring proudly and for quite some time. I got a new outfit, shoes, and flowers for their wedding. It was a simple ceremony. The church was packed with friends and family, all rejoicing and excited to see how God had blessed both Mom and me with a wonderful, loving husband and father.

Walt made sure that I was included on the second honeymoon, in Virginia Beach, Virginia. We have home movies of that time that show me playing a hiding game around the pool with my new daddy. I had never stayed in a hotel before, and I loved jumping back and forth from bed to bed.

It was also my first time at the ocean, and I discovered that my new daddy loved the ocean. He taught me how to ride the waves, build sand castles, and bury ourselves in the sand. I remember proudly announcing to the waiters and waitresses we met on that trip, "We're on our honeymoon!" Mom was embarrassed, of course, but a feeling of belonging and a sense of family was forming in me. From the very beginning, I was included in everything, just as if I was Walt's very own. A few short months after their marriage, Daddy adopted me, and I legally became his and took his name.

My mother married and I was adopted into a wonderful, new, loving family. The Lord had given me another daddy and grandmother who embraced me with love and kindness. Mom says I adjusted well to this new environment, but somewhere deep inside I was still sad and had a sense of loss in my spirit. Without knowing it, a sort of turmoil was going on inside me.

Before my mother had remarried, people would sometimes talk about my biological father if I asked about him. However, once we became a new family unit, the subject of my biological father was seldom mentioned. I could ask questions, but everyone's behavior communicated to me that it was time to move on. I loved my new daddy, and about a year later excitedly welcomed my new baby sister.

The adults around me thought I seemed to be adjusting into my role as part of this new family unit. And I would agree on many levels I was. For the first time, my mom could be at home with me. She no longer needed to work, and I know that made her so happy. One of the recurring memories I have, and that I am grateful for, are all the times I would come home from school and mom was there to just talk. We spent many hours after school talking about the day and all sorts of things. I loved those times, and they made me feel so good. My mom also was able to be the homemaker she desired. She was great at this. We always had family dinners together, she loved to decorate the house and move furniture around, and she sewed all our clothes when we were young. I learned so many things from her, how to entertain, how to sew, how to cook and decorate a home. And when I married I brought these values into my family as a wife and mother the best I knew how.

However, there were unanswered questions in my heart. I kept them secret, not wanting to hurt mom or my new daddy's feelings or disrupt this wonderful new life. An area of hurt and grief that I never resolved was left in my heart, along with misunderstandings.

A New Daddy and a New Family

I have never referred to my new daddy as my stepfather, nor did I ever see him that way. We had a great relationship right from the start. I have always referred to my biological father as Carl and Walt as my daddy. In my heart, Walt is my daddy and Carl gave me life. Walt was the daddy who fathered me through my childhood.

From the beginning Walt's family accepted me as one of their own. I instantly had uncles and aunts, another grandma, and lots of cousins. It was a fun family, a family who loved being together and sharing adventures. My dad had a cottage, complete with a speed boat, on a lake in Conneaut, Pennsylvania. One of my uncles had a pick-up truck, and all the cousins would get in the back and ride down to the boat docks to swim, fish, or take our turn at water skiing. We spent many summer weekends there. I learned to water ski there and loved it. My dad was a great water skier, excelling on the slalom ski and the round disc. I remember being in the boat watching with amazement as he did various tricks. I wanted to learn to ski like he did.

Most of my cousins were older, and they treated me like I'd always been with them. Two older girl cousins would take me bicycle riding with them on a two-seater bike. I climbed trees with the boys and swung on the rope that hung from the trees. There was always something happening when we were at the cottage with all the family.

Dad also owned a hunting cabin. It truly was a guys' hunting cabin with an outhouse and all, but I can recall several occasions when we were all there. One night while we cousins slept on bunk beds in one big room, we thought we heard mice in the cabin. We squealed with laughter, thinking they might nibble on our toes or crawl into our warm sleeping bags as we slept.

A freezing cold mountain creek flowed beside the cabin, where we washed ourselves and brushed our teeth. There was no running water in the cabin, but I loved it. Dad's family loved to hunt and they taught us all how to shoot at targets. I also learned how to shoot a bow and arrow. As I learned how to handle a bow and arrow correctly, I had some good scrapes on my arms from the string. I decided it was harder than firing a gun.

We took walks and rides through the mountains of Pennsylvania. I fell in love with the woods and the trees and watching the animals. The family often went deer spotting at night in the pick-up truck. We had a big spotlight and would find herds of deer, try to count the racks on them, and see if we could find the does with their fawns.

We had campfires and cookouts at both the cottage and the cabin. Those times where the entire family gathered were exciting and totally new experiences for this little girl.

Adventures and experiences never stopped. At age 12, I learned how to ride a dirt bike. Almost everyone in Daddy's family rode except Grandma, Mom, and my aunts. When it was my turn to learn to ride, Daddy bought a new sparkly emerald green Honda 100. I had my share of wrecks, including running into our van while it was parked in the driveway and denting the fender. Daddy never angered easily and was always more concerned about me getting injured than the damage I did to the toys we were enjoying. I loved to ride that bike in the woods beside our house. We had trails that could take us over a mile away. I loved being outdoors in nature and in the woods.

Camping, fishing, and canoeing were also big loves of my dad's. We went on short camping trips from March through October just about every year. I was allowed to bring friends on some of those trips and that always made them more fun. We cooked out, sat by the campfire, went for walks, visited nearby parks, and went sight-seeing. Sometimes we would haul the boat to Raystown Lake, where we fished, skied, and lived on the boat all day long. My dad was an outdoorsman at heart. I know this is where I received my love and appreciation for the outdoors.

When I was about nine years old, I told my mom and dad that I wanted to learn to play the piano. Dad bought me a brand-new piano, and I took nine years of lessons from an amazing classical piano teacher. My mom and dad would often ask me to play for guests, family, and friends who visited. They even followed me through the Teen Talent competitions I entered every year through our church youth group. I still have that piano and a great love for music.

It's All About the Horses!

We had an amazing three-sided family, my mother's, my dad's, and Carl's, with all three sides loving and caring for the other. There was never any fighting or jealousy that existed. They valued the role that each played in the story that brought our lives together.

Carl's sister, my aunt Judi, owned horses and taught me how to ride and to care for them when I would visit her place in Dubose, Pennsylvania. I loved going there in the summer and being with her and my grandparents on the farm and tending the horses. Aunt Judi had three quarter horses named Missy, Misty, and Harmen. I got to name Misty when she was foaled based on a book I was reading at the time about a horse named Misty.

My aunt taught me how to saddle and ride. I loved riding with her through the fields around her place and down the country roads. I remember the first time I was allowed to saddle the pony and ride around the property by myself. The pony was sweet and reliable and never really did anything out of the ordinary. However, I must not have cinched the saddle right, and part way through our ride, I slid sideways off the pony and onto the ground, saddle and all. The pony just kept on going, heading right back to her stall in the barn. I still had a lot to learn about horseback riding, but I had fallen in love with horses and dreamed that one day I would own one of my own.

I think my favorite vacation was the summer when Dad, Mom, my sister, and I headed out with no particular plan as to our destination. We landed on Chincoteague Island, Virginia, just in time for the swim of the wild horses. Every year wild horses from the island swim to the mainland. I was in horse heaven! We spent a week there enjoying the shore and the festivities that surrounded the old traditions of the wild horse yearly swim. My mom and daddy even let me put my name in the raffle to win one of the horses from the swim. I clung to the hope that I would win one of those beautiful wild horses, not giving any thought to where we would keep the horse. Daddy let me dream and hope and even believe that I could win. He never mentioned anything about the reality of winning. He just let me enjoy the moment. I didn't win, of course, but that year the vacation was all about horses, a memory for a lifetime was formed.

My Dad, the Carpenter

My dad was a carpenter by trade, and an amazing one at that. He made lots of our furniture, and I can remember the smell of sawed lumber filling the house from the workshop in the basement. He taught me how to use his tools, and I assisted him with small projects around the house. When our roof needed to be replaced, he helped me onto the roof, and I helped with some of the job. Daddy still does most of the repairs around the house; he's amazing!

Daddy built two sets of bedroom furniture, one for me, one for my sister. He let me give him ideas about its design so I would have plenty of shelves for my horse books and pictures. One Christmas, he made a huge doll house with rooms and furniture. My mom, an excellent seamstress, made clothes for the dolls and other items that filled the house. It was fantastic! My sister and I loved that house and played with it often.

Later, after Ken and I married and were expecting our first child, I wanted a crib and dresser combo; and Daddy made me exactly what I wanted. I used it for all three of our children and then passed it on to my sister for her two children.

Daddy Showed Me Unconditional Love

It still brings tears to my eyes when I think of the blessing of my dad. This man's huge heart of love for us left a great impact on my life. I can honestly say this man never wounded me in any way. He loved me unconditionally and gave me a childhood I would have never had without him.

In one of my prayer times, the Lord spoke to me about His adoption of us into the family of God. He reminded me of my dad's adoption of me and the response of his family. I was welcomed and grafted into my dad's family with no questions asked and no distinctions made. It was as if I was born into his family, and my place was secured. That's what our heavenly Father has done for us through His Son. My dad was a tangible, physical example of the spiritual principle of adoption into God's family. What a blessing from God, when He gave me my dad!

Thanks, Daddy, for your amazing care, love, and nurture. I can never repay you and I will always be grateful, for you showed the love of Christ through your fathering.

Aunt Judi's Observations After the Adoption

I really have no recollection of seeing any change in Chrystal in her younger years, or the onset of any problems. She appeared to adjust well when Dolores and Walt married, and he was a warm and loving father from the beginning. Chrystal never opened up or revealed much of herself, preferring to be a private person. She didn't share much of her inner self with anyone, though she seemed close to my mother, her grandmother, who had helped to raise her.[1]

Hiding Games

When I first met Walt, I would hide, unsure about why he was coming around. He played along with the game and eventually I realized I was safe with him. Later I would play the hiding game with others, family and friends. I became very good at hiding, using the same mind-set to hide that part of me I didn't want anyone to see and the part I didn't want to see.

As an adult, I adapted my skills at "hiding games." As adults, these games take on a whole new dimension. Running away from difficulties, masking our broken and wounded hearts, pretending that we are in control when we have lost our grip, we hide the person we really are. We project the image of what we think we should be so we will be accepted and affirmed by others.

The problem I found with playing these "hiding games" was that hiding places were inadequate. While offering me a quick fix, the hiding places never really dealt with the heart of the problem. We look for avenues that offer momentary diversion when we don't want to deal with real life. After the moment in time, as soon as we venture out, the pain is right there waiting. The truth is that our hiding places only complicate the issues in the long run, as we're never forced to face the cause of the problem.

When we move into adulthood, our childish hiding games manifest in other ways. They include: performing, withdrawing, excessive shopping sprees, overeating, or other such self-destructive behaviors. Drugs and alcohol are often used to drown the pain and responsibilities we sense are too great to carry.

Appearing friendly and giving the illusion that I had my act together, I hid behind humor and laughter. Self-debasing humor is often an attempt to beat others to the punch, giving us a sense of control over our own shortcomings.

These and many more hiding places are diversions used to keep us from dealing with the true issues of our hearts. We hide because we hurt. When that first inkling of pain crops up, we run to a self-indulging spot, rather than to Jesus. These self-indulging places always increase our dissatisfaction with ourselves, others, and life in general. It is not wrong to hide, but where we hide will either help or hurt us. That is why Jesus asks us to leave our hiding places and hide ourselves in Him. Only He can truly shelter us. At the same time, He helps us to deal with the true issues of the heart. He is the only one who can fill our empty lives with meaning, when we seek refuge in Him instead of running away from reality and playing our hiding games.

> I knew Chrystal in high school. As a matter of fact we were best friends. I used to go camping with them. We both loved to water ski and be outdoors. We had sleepovers at each other's houses and hung out together doing all those things teenage girls do together. I remember one time when she gave me a perm, which was fun while we were doing it, but it convinced me of the value of having a professional do it from then on. She was definitely the stronger of the two of us. I backslid at one time in my life and she was right there for me, praying for me. She never lectured or judged me. She was a friend no matter what I did. I was totally shocked when I learned about her mental illness. I even felt guilty,

thinking what a terrible friend I was not to have seen what she was going through. She definitely did a good job of hiding the pain she was feeling from all of us. The only thing I remember she ever did that had to do with her biological father was read his Bible. She showed it to me one time when I was there for a sleepover. She always seemed to get along great with her parents and her sister. We have always tried to get together whenever she is in town but sometimes it just doesn't work out. I do remember when she came home for her grandfather's funeral, though. She called me and said she needed me to be there with her. I went with her to the funeral and to the gravesite. It was really hard for her to let go that day. She wanted to stay until they lowered the casket into the ground so I stayed with her until she was ready to leave. It was a really hard time for her.[2]

Broken Perspective

To give people an idea of what living this kind of life was like for me, I often tell this story. A young child lived in a house that had only one window. One day, someone threw rocks at the window, damaged the glass, causing the child's perspective to be distorted. Because of this distorted view of life, a variety of harmful emotions took root in that child's heart.

First of all, the damaged window affected the child's ability to see clearly through the viewing window. Now, when this child looked at people, circumstances, and even God, everything looked distorted and threatening. Second, when this child used the window as a mirror to evaluate his or her value, the reflection was of a broken image.

The adults in this child's life did not understand the child's broken perspective. They couldn't give the direction, protection, and correction that he or she needed. The child developed a shattered ability to trust.

Without trust, in order to feel safe, we try to be in control of the circumstances around us. However, people and circumstances are unpredictable, a constant threat to our security. We begin to develop our own way to deal with the confusion this causes in our lives. To keep people from seeing who we truly are inside, many of us resort to suppressing our feelings and wearing masks we have designed for ourselves.

When my biological father died, somehow my "window to the world" became distorted. With this distortion, I developed a deepseated lack of trust. Eventually manifesting in one form or another in all of my relationships, I became an expert at developing intricate masks. Those masks projected who I wanted to be and effectively hid what I didn't want anyone else to see. I thought I had a pretty good Christian mask in place that would impress everyone, including God. I never realized that constantly wearing masks caused me to begin to lose who I really was and who God had designed me to be. This caused problems with every relationship in my life.

Looking into the condition of our inner world can be difficult. Adam and Eve covered up out of shame and hid, but out of love God pursued them (see Genesis 3:7-9). He desires a relationship with us and has made provision for our sin. But we must first acknowledge we are hiding and call out to Him even in those shameful and hurtful places. Today, would you allow Him in? Begin by praying and asking God to reveal areas of your life that you developed masks to hide. You can pray this:

Heavenly Father, I know I have hidden behind masks because of shame, fear, or guilt. I am tired of hiding and need You desperately. Today I invited You in and ask You to help me live fully in You without my masks.

My Adventure and Journey With God

1. Think about your growing up years from age six through adolescence. Do you remember any particularly positive or negative events? What was your relationship with your parents at this time in your life? Briefly describe them.

2. When thinking of the description of hiding, how good were you or are you at hiding games and can you list what you may have chosen to hide?

3. What was your relationship with God during this time in your life? Did you hide from God like Adam and Eve? What were you hiding or what are you hiding from God?

4. Often, the result of hiding a part of ourselves is performance. Do you believe you had a performance bent in your character and how has that manifested?

5. You may have discovered some areas where forgiveness is required between you and a family member. Be open to allow the Lord to show you where you need to forgive someone because of the hurt they caused. Remember that forgiveness is a command of the Lord not an option (see Mark 11:25). And that forgiveness frees you and allows your heart to heal. Forgiveness is a joint effort between you and God, your willingness to forgive and His strength

to do the rest (see Colossians 3:13). It is not about establishing trust with the offender, for that can only happen through appropriate relationship building. Here is a sample prayer to help you, say this prayer for as many people that you need to forgive:

Heavenly Father, I confess my choice to harbor unforgiveness in my heart. I see the need for me to release (name this person) and forgive them for (name what they did). I choose to forgive and ask for Your help. Heal the pain that was caused from this situation and allow me to walk freely in Your love and forgiveness toward me (see Matthew 6:12). Amen.

6. Scriptures to continue to pray and meditate on: Psalm 51:10-12; Psalm 32:1-5; Psalm 19:12-14.

CHAPTER 4

WEARING MASKS

RAISED IN A WONDERFUL CHRISTIAN HOME, brought up going to church, I remember giving my heart to the Lord at about the age of four. Activities kept me busy, and I loved every moment of them. After graduating from high school, I went off to Bible school. I loved the Lord with my whole heart and wanted to serve and please Him with everything in me.

Outwardly I was happy, carefree, and had lots of friends. I portrayed a confidence that conveyed to everyone that I knew where I was going and was in control of my life. Everyone thought I would go far in life. However, because of my inner struggles, a well-developed mask had formed over my heart.

Chrystal was a great college roommate! She was bubbly and loved the Lord and was intent on serving Him. She was a very happy person. She spoke of her family often. She spoke of her biological father, Carl, and how he passed away and how she would have loved to have known him but also felt so loved and cared for by her dad, Walt. She never spoke of him as her stepfather. You really would have never known that Walt was not her father. Their relationship was sweet and her family was wonderful.[1]

On the inside, the relentless turmoil prevailed. I remember crying myself to sleep some nights feeling the pain of a loss that I didn't understand. How could I be grieving for someone I had never known? How could I miss a father I had never even seen? How could I want a parent who had never held me in his arms? I replayed these questions over and over in my mind, yet I couldn't answer them. I was afraid to ask questions because I feared they weren't relevant. The plain fact was that I had never physically known my father, yet the pain and emotions in my heart were strong and left me confused and hurt. I learned quickly that there was no point in trying to discuss this part of my life with anyone else, so I kept it hidden behind my masks hoping it would go away and never return.

I tried to suppress these thoughts. Whenever I achieved anything or experienced milestones in my life, I wondered what Carl would have thought. I wondered what my relationship with him might have been like. When I was left alone I thought about those things. I could feel the pain of a loss that I really didn't understand. I would cry out to the Lord to give me understanding. God's silence and my inability to move past or through this inner turmoil frustrated me.

I did all the things I had been taught. I read the Word, worshiped, and spent time in prayer. Yet these activities acted as a Band-Aid rather than a cure for my heart. As a result, I buried these feelings and questions deeper and deeper in the recesses of my heart. Rather than openly dealing with them, I wore either a confidence or performance mask.

My Performance Mask

I had wonderful experiences with the Lord. In my church community I was exposed to great moves of God, great speakers and healing evangelists who would come through our area. I decided that I wanted to give my life to the Lord in ministry. Growing up in the church, I learned all the dos and don'ts of Christianity. I complied with all the "acceptable" behaviors I'd been taught, such as not going to the movies or wearing pants to church. I actually learned I should perform, then God would do His part. I thought that God would do things in my life because I was a good Christian girl.

Even when I was doing my best to be a good Christian, I couldn't get relief from this inner sadness and struggle. Christians hardly talked about inner struggles. I never heard sermons about how to deal with them. Instead we heard how we were to rejoice in the Lord and that the joy of the Lord would be our strength. If we had not yet reached that place in our lives, we were instructed to read Scripture, praise a little more, and head to the altar to be prayed for and pray it through. I tried all of that. Yet I was still left with an inward struggle and had no answers as to why there was such unrest in my heart and in my life.

Others seemed to solve their problems in the prescribed way, and I decided there must be something wrong with me. Obviously I was not trying hard enough. I became a really good performer. I became an expert at wearing masks to conceal my inner feelings. One very effective mask was, "I'm having lots of fun and enjoying life." This fooled even those closest to me. My self-assurance mask conveyed that I had my act together and could handle whatever came my way in life.

GOD CAN YOU LOVE ME

Nobody, not even my best friends, had a clue as to what was really going on inside of my heart. In truth, I was a confused, insecure person with low self-esteem. I figured there was something wrong with me because I had been taught all my life about the "faith train." A Christian was supposed to have the faith for whatever the need. Eventually his/her feelings and emotions would come along behind. I was to step out in faith and then my feelings would catch up. But for me, that never happened, and it left me confused about my real identity.

What's Wrong With Me?

When we lie down to rest each night, the inner thoughts and issues of our mind and heart often surface. In my case that was where I would wrestle the most, trying desperately to make sense of the inner struggle versus the reality of a wonderful family and a good godly upbringing. I battled with wondering what was wrong with me. If God was answering my prayers, as everyone told me He would, why couldn't I hear Him? Why did it seem like the joy of the Lord was for everyone but me? I kept hanging on and waiting for the day my prayers would be answered. Meanwhile, I stayed in performance mode.

My thought process led me to believe that if I would just do a little more, maybe I'd feel better. If I would just study the Word a little bit more, then maybe I'd be all right. I already felt I was called into ministry, so I decided to throw myself into that and give myself to the work of the Lord. I believed that by doing all of these things, my feelings would eventually come around, and the questions would go away. But that never happened, and I had to develop more and better masks to keep my pain and confusion hidden until I could figure out what I was doing wrong. I became an overachiever, set unreasonable goals for myself, and did everything I could think of to achieve inner peace with myself, God, and my life.

My sister and I are six years apart and she left for college when I was entering middle school. She hardly lived at home again after she left for college (in Missouri) and then she married and moved away. As a teenager, she often spent a lot of time alone in her bedroom. My memories are that she always seemed to want to be alone reading her Bible and praying in her room. As the little sister, I would try to get her attention and very much wanted to spend time with her. However, I never felt that she really wanted much to do with me.[2]

The sad part about depression is the fact that it affects every relationship in your life in one form or another. The day some of my mother's friends had a baby shower for my mom and new baby sister, I was sent off to kindergarten. However, I never made it there. I hid in the bushes outside of our house because I wanted to be at the party and not go to school. Everyone thought it was funny and sweet, and I was able to stay home that day and enjoy the festivities. Just like having a new daddy in my life was an adjustment, so was having a new baby sister.

I remember holding my sister after she was born and wearing a mask to protect her from catching my cold I had at that time. I vividly remember the thoughts that raced through my mind as I gazed at that sweet little innocent face, *Mommy and my new daddy now have their own little girl, and now they are a family.* For whatever reason I could not embrace the "we are a family" in that moment; it was "they are a family now." Sadly, I believe that mind-set created a wall between us and created an unspoken distance during our early years as sisters. Later I would regret what was lost during those years.

Everyone knows that teenagers go through major changes as they move from childhood into puberty. I look back now and see that I was actually beginning to go through what would later be diagnosed as depression. I remember as I went through junior high and then high school, there were times I preferred to be alone when my friends from the neighborhood wanted to do something. My excuse would be that I had too much homework, but the constant sadness that I couldn't shake was sometimes difficult to hide so I would withdraw until I felt I had it under control.

At other times my activity was characteristic of what is now known as bipolar. I would experience long bouts of extremely high energy levels and feelings of excitement where I could get a lot done, often going without sleep. Suddenly I would come to a dead stop and I would need to sleep or rest. I would be lethargic and really sad for days and hide until those feelings would pass. I would repeat the cycle moving at high levels of activity until the next crash came. Family and friends never really picked up on it because the pattern fit into the expected behavior or profile of a teenager.

The Warrior Is a Child

Does anyone really live in a way that's fully transparent? I think not. Most of us try hard to master the behaviors that bring acceptance, while struggling with our inner thoughts and feelings of inadequacy and insecurity. Since Carl's death occurred before I was born, the adults in my life had no clue concerning the confusion I was experiencing. I was puzzled over what I was feeling since it made no logical sense to me. I covered up my true feelings and hid all the while, secretly hoping that by ignoring those feelings they would just vanish. My greatest fear was that if I voiced my thoughts I would cause my dad great hurt and pain. I didn't want him to think I didn't love him, so I kept silent.

I was known as a confident, self-assured, and carefree young woman. Most perceived me as a strong leader who was able to manage several tasks at once. While I appeared calm, together, and in control on the outside, underneath I was a frightened, sad, insecure child. Years ago, Twila Paris released a song called "The Warrior Is a Child." When I heard the words I thought it was an accurate depiction of who I was: a confident warrior in appearance, but a lonely, scared, and hurting child inside.

The Warrior Is a Child

Lately I've been winning battles left and right,
But even winners can get wounded in the fight.
People say that I'm amazing
Strong beyond my years,
But they don't see inside of me
I'm hiding all the tears.

They don't know that I go running home when I fall down.
They don't know who picks me up when no one is around.
I drop my sword and cry for just a while,
'Cause deep inside this armor
The warrior is a child.

Unafraid because His armor is the best.
But even soldiers need a quiet place to rest.
People say that I'm amazing,
Never face retreat.
But they don't see the enemies
That lay me at His feet.

I drop my sword and look up for His smile,
Because deep inside this armor

Deep inside this armor
Deep inside this armor
The warrior is a child.[5]

My Adventure and Journey With God

1. Again think honestly about your inner life and reread "The Warrior is a Child." Are you seeing any masks? If so, what kind of masks are you wearing to conceal the real you?

2. Are there hidden areas in your life that you feel would cause others to judge you or dislike you if they knew the truth about you?

3. Have you ever felt like you had to earn the love of a parent? Or have you ever felt you had to earn God's love? Briefly journal your thoughts.

4. Reflect on what God's Word says about His love for you? Read John 3:16. How much do you feel God loves you?

5. Read one Psalm a day this week and record them below. What do you discover? And do you think David felt that God was not hearing and answering his prayers?

6. Write out a verse or two from the Psalms that you feel accurately describes the way you are feeling right now. Confidently pray these back to the Lord.

7. Read Psalm 62:5-8 and wait quietly before Him.

CHAPTER 5

MARRIAGE AND MINISTRY

UPON ENTERING BIBLE COLLEGE in Springfield, Missouri, I moved confidently ahead with my preparation for full-time ministry. I was elected to the student council for the freshman class, and that's where Ken first noticed me. A few months later, a mutual friend set us up to go to a basketball game together as a first date.

I remember she was totally focused on going into full-time ministry as a woman evangelist. She made it clear she wasn't interested in a serious relationship. I really didn't see her again until she came back after going on a missions outreach for spring break. I had given her a card and a stuffed animal wishing her a great spring break. We dated from March to August and then began a two-year engagement that lasted until I graduated. We had a great relationship until Chrystal went home to get ready for the wedding while I finished my senior year. It was hard for her to be at home with me in Missouri. She began to show signs of jealousy, but I just chalked it up to the stress of preparing for our wedding.[1]

We were married in 1984. Ken was 22, and I was 21. We were married one weekend and started our first ministry position the next weekend. Something happened once we made the commitment and said our vows. Suddenly, I began to have feelings in the context of my relationship with my husband that I was sure were not normal. I would have bouts of jealousy followed by bouts of rage. I was deathly afraid that he was going to leave me or die. It was all very confusing to me. Even though I had dealt with sadness in the past, I considered myself a very upbeat person. I was always an optimist, a glass-half-full kind of person. When feelings of rage, anger, jealousy, and insecurity began to surface, I was shocked. Where in the world were they coming from? My first thought was that there was something my husband was not doing that would have given me the security I needed in our marriage relationship.

The church situation where we were working didn't help our marriage at all. We became the youth pastors for a church in Ohio where we stayed for the next three years. This church had been through numerous staff changes in the years prior to our coming. The leadership was not easy to work with and was really not in favor of women in ministry, so a lot of hurt was incurred during our time there. All these issues added stress to our shaky, young marital relationship.

When Ken and Chrystal first came to our church as young youth pastors, our daughters were a part of the youth group, so we naturally desired to get to know them. Our first impression of Chrystal was that she appeared to be scared and ministry wasn't what she thought it would be. Over time we became very good friends, inviting them often to our home for meals and card games. Our relationship grew to the point where we mentored them as they shared their concerns and struggles about ministry and marriage. We knew things were difficult on many fronts and we just tried to encourage and have fun in the midst of it all. We never imagined what was beneath the struggles or what their journey would entail. We knew we had found friends for a lifetime.[2]

Out of Control

During our first years of marriage, I found myself erupting into fits of jealous rage. At times I would hit my head against the wall or punch the countertops to alleviate my anger and insecurity about our relationship. I was shocked by what was coming out of me. I thought I had always been a very rational person. I had never felt or expressed this type of anger and rage before. The emotions became so intense that I would throw things as hard as I could to try to release the pressure building up inside of me. Though I was angry, I was scared to death over what was happening to me.

At the time I thought it must be Ken's fault. If he was the kind of husband that he needed to be, then I wouldn't be experiencing such intense jealousy and insecurity. We tried to work through what looked like an insecurity issue in me. We felt we had identified the problem and didn't feel it was anything abnormal. Ken, who is a very even-keeled and understanding person, patiently tried to help me overcome my insecurities.

"I couldn't figure out what happened to the happy-go-lucky girl I had married," Ken shares. "It was quite bizarre. Chrystal had taken a receptionist job at Emerge Ministries, a Christian counseling center, so I thought she ought to talk to someone there."

We actually went into the initial counseling sessions thinking that Ken just needed to learn how to reassure me of our relationship. Dr. Dobbins, founder of Emerge Ministries, talked to us both and then told Ken it was an "issue" with me. It caught us both by surprise when we found it was a deep-seeded, unresolved issue in me that was the real problem.

Christian Counseling

As Dr. Dobbins listened to me talk about my past, he told us he felt there was something going on with my heart that had to do with my biological father passing away. That was the first time any light began to shine on the sorrow buried deep inside my heart. I never realized that the sadness I had experienced all my life was caused by the pain in my heart from not knowing my biological father. The result of unresolved grief was now interfering in my marriage relationship.

I was able to perform some cognitive processing exercises that Dr. Dobbins taught me. When I felt my emotions were getting out of hand, I could adjust and get myself back on track. Along my journey, though, I had adopted a wrong belief. I thought that through sheer determination and good Christian disciplines, I could overcome the sadness and despair I felt deep inside. As I entered my late twenties and early thirties, my determination began to wane. I was growing tired of the fight, and my masks became almost too heavy to lift into place each Sunday morning. It became harder and harder to maintain the image I had created for myself. What would I do if the masks could no longer hide my internal struggles? What if others could see the cracks in my armor that I had been working so hard to conceal all my life?

Thank You, God, for Rock Island

Ken remembers those tough first three years of marriage and how frustrating it was trying to serve God in that situation:

> I was at the point of resigning from ministry altogether when, out of the blue, a church in Rock Island, Illinois, called to offer me a position as youth pastor. It was incredible! The senior pastor called and told me they had been praying about offering the position to us after four or five people had told him we were the ones God wanted in that position. He said the job was mine if I wanted it. I have to be honest and say I was more than a little gun-shy after what we had been through the past three years. Chrystal and I talked it over and decided to go check it out.
>
> What we found was a dream world. These people loved us back to life. Chrystal thrived there. She was placed over the young adult and young married ministry. The senior pastor was absolutely thrilled with what she was doing. She started to bloom there, and the fits of jealousy and rage began to subside. We continued to implement the tools Dr. Dobbins had given us and our relationship with each other seemed to improve dramatically.[3]

Superwoman

We started our family five years into our marriage. We were still at the wonderful church in Rock Island when our first son, Ryan, was born. Our daughter, Reneé, came 17 months later. We happily celebrated these blessed births, but the sadness of my heart had not completely gone away; and with the move into parenthood, the unresolved grief I had been suppressing began to resurface and intensify. I could feel the mood swings coming on again, so I tried twice as hard to counter them. I reasoned that being a young mother of two small children was probably why I was battling this again. Nevertheless, I was committed to being the wife, mother, and minister God had called me to be.

I was determined to continue in ministry and never let the enemy have the victory. There was a very strong-willed part of me that wasn't going to give up. I determined that it was a fight for my life, and I was not going to lose. Most people had no idea what was really going on inside of me. Those around me began to tell me they thought I was a superwoman as I sped through life at hyper speed, running from one project to another while still caring for my young children and maintaining a very full ministry schedule. Comments of amazement from others only showed me how well I had been able to mask what I was really going through. That gave me a level of comfort, but the energy and determination it took to maintain this image began to take its toll on me physically, mentally, and spiritually.

I Was Losing Myself

What seems to have happened to me was that I began a slow backward progression. As infants, our motor and neurological skills develop through reaching toward our parents and families that surround us. Then we start developing our thinking and learn how to relate to other people in the social realm. If we are raised in a Christian home, like I was, around age four we are introduced to the spiritual realm and begin learning about the Lord and how we need Him in our life. This basically describes a kind of natural progression of development as we move from infancy to adulthood.

I began to regress and I lost these skills almost in the same order as one would normally gain them. The first thing that was threatened was my spiritual walk. I had been taught there was a certain way to gain victory in our Christian walk. I was not experiencing victory while I was following what was considered standard operating procedure. I experienced a serious crisis of faith where I began to ask myself if God was really who He said He was. I couldn't hear Him during worship or when I read the Bible. I didn't want someone preaching at me or praying for me because I didn't see any results. My foundation of faith began to deteriorate. I thought I had believed a lie all my life or that God was very cruel and uncaring.

Once the foundation I was raised on was called into question, I didn't know how to relate to other Christians. Because I was in a state of confusion about the God factor in my life, I began to retreat from social activities. This extended into other areas of my life. I couldn't think straight or respond appropriately. With my impaired thinking I was not able to do simple tasks or accomplish everyday routines. I was falling farther and farther away from normal life activities that I loved and enjoyed.

During times of depression, I became physically lethargic and didn't want to move. I wanted to curl up in a ball and wrap my blankets around me. I didn't like who I was becoming, but I didn't seem to be able to do anything about it. Ken and I began to wonder if we were to continue in ministry. Had we missed God completely?

My Adventure and Journey With God

1. As you read this part of Chrystal's life story, did you see a pattern beginning to develop? Does this resonate with any of your life patterns?

2. Did you have any unresolved issues with your earthly father? If yes, describe them.

3. How did your relationship with your earthly father affect your marriage relationship?

4. How do you feel about talking with a counselor about any problems you may perceive in either your marriage relationship or your relationship with your parents? Contact a spiritual advisor or pastor and ask for a recommendation.

5. Have you used any of the following "self-preservation" tactics to avoid dealing with painful relationships? Circle the ones that apply to you.

   Control

   Ignore

   Withdraw

   Blame

   Denial

   Passive/Aggressive Behavior

6. Read Psalm 68:4-5 and Psalm 27:10. Allow these verses to comfort you. What kind of relationship do you think David might have had with his earthly father?

7. How has your relationship with your earthly father impacted your relationship with your heavenly Father? Sometimes the way we feel about our earthly dads can

mirror our feelings with our heavenly dad. Our struggles can reflect far more than our battle with people or events. They often reveal questions about God's faithfulness, provision, or love. List any questions on your heart. Then take time to ask God those questions and allow Him time to answer you.

8. Now read Second Corinthians 6:18. Pray and ask your heavenly Father to confirm this promise in your heart.

CHAPTER 6

CRACKS IN THE ARMOR

IN 1992, MY HUSBAND became a senior pastor, after eight years of youth and young adult ministries. Excited, as well as challenged, we moved to Bolingbrook, a suburb of Chicago. We felt this was where God wanted us, though knowing the church had experienced a split and had serious financial problems. Now I was the senior pastor's wife, in a brand-new church community, as well as the mother of two small children.

Ken remembers what those first few years were like at Living Water Church.

We worked at building a foundation in the church and saw it grow from about 150 to 250 people. In 1994 we went to two services, offering a contemporary first service and a more traditional second service. The board had hired a lay person to oversee the music ministry after the church split who was more comfortable with the traditional type of music. Chrystal, who is very talented musically, led the praise and worship for the contemporary service. The popularity of the contemporary service caused a power struggle, which ended with the traditional music director leaving the church, taking most of the music department with him. This made our roles as senior pastors even more difficult.[1]

We were working on putting ministry teams together and building a staff when our third child, Eric, was born. I now had three small children at home plus the responsibilities of being a pastor's wife. A lot was happening in our lives, so when I continued to experience the extreme highs and lows, we thought it was just exhaustion. Labeling it as burnout, I took three months off from all church responsibilities. But in that three-month time, instead of getting better, I got worse, and the move toward a total collapse got closer.

I knew Ken and Chrystal when they first came to Living Water Community Church. I was only 21 and newly married. I remember my first impression of Chrystal, the new pastor's wife, was that she seemed to have it all together. She was always doing things, always busy but never frazzled. I started working as an administrative assistant, and one day we were talking about the upcoming Christmas season. Chrystal told me she always makes her three kids pajamas for Christmas. I had sewed some but I remember thinking that was the neatest thing. I asked her how she found the time to get that done with everything else she was doing. She said she would either do it all in one day on a day off or stay up all night Christmas Eve to finish them.

Another thing I remember as I look back is when we had this church craft show where people could set up booths to sell their homemade crafts. Chrystal set up her booth on the day of the event, seemingly out of the blue. She had made these amazing baskets out of fabric, a lot of them. When we asked how she had put this all together so quickly with three little kids, she said, "Oh, I just worked on them and got them done." We were all thinking she was this supermom, this superwoman who could do anything. She was so together and seemed to get everything done. When Ken and the elders came and told us about Chrystal's illness, we were all floored. Not her, she's so together, this can't be possible! It was unfathomable and hard to understand.[2]

My husband would sense when something was wrong, especially if he came home and found I had slept all afternoon. As I began to reveal a little more of what was going on in my head to him, I would become more and more agitated. I didn't understand why I was thinking and acting like that when I didn't want to be that way. Why didn't I seem to be able to be the kind of person that I wanted to be? I felt like this thing was beginning to take control of me. Whatever it was it was trying to control my emotions, my moods, and my level of activity. I had a very strong determination to fight through it and not let it deprive me of a normal productive life.

The ups and downs began to get more and more severe and started to disrupt my life. Whenever I was down, I couldn't minister or pray for people. I would retreat and tell people I needed a little bit of a break. I would take a month off, try to do the thinking exercises I had been taught in our earlier counseling sessions, and made a determined attempt to get my life back on track. It was similar to the pattern I had experienced as a teenager, but now it was magnified. A lot more people were affected by my mood swings because now I was a wife, a mother, and a minister.

As this unpredictable journey progressed, we were met with hurdles that quickly escalated to major obstacles. Not fully knowing how to handle and deal with various situations, I saw my stability as a leader, believer, wife, and mother begin to deteriorate. Within six years, that deterioration infected every area of my life. At 33 years of age, I found myself heading for a complete mental collapse.

By the spring of 1995, everything was changing for the worst. I questioned every spiritual aspect of my being and doubted my relationship with God. The search for reasons and answers became insurmountable to the point of complete and utter despair. I never thought I could be so severely shaken to the core of my belief system. I wasn't even sure if God truly wanted me as His child or loved me like His Word said. I went into an uncontrollable tailspin, and the pressure increased to the point that I was no longer able to live and function as a wife, mother, or minister.

Crisis of Faith

In January 1996, I noticed an inward breaking that I had no words to describe. I was scared to death about what I was feeling and sensing. Frantically I searched for ways to relieve the pressure by relinquishing responsibilities at the church and trying to find time to rest during my daily routines. I would go on small trips and spend time away to refocus, but no relief came. My days were clouded with confusion and feelings of disorientation.

I began to experience memory loss, both short and long term. I could not focus or concentrate on the simplest task. What was I to wear, to eat, or what was I to do next? To complete a simple task became utter agony. I lost the mental ability to think, to choose, to reason, to will, to be. In that period I so identified with the Psalmist's anguish in Psalm 18:4-6: *"The cords of death entangled me; the torrents of destruction overwhelmed me. The cords of the grave coiled around me; the snares of death confronted me. In my distress I called to the Lord; I cried to my God for help."* I hoped that God was with me; I knew He heard my cries; but I heard nothing, saw nothing, and still had little explanation as to what was happening to me.

All my life I had been taught that faith without works is dead. If I could just put my faith into action, I reasoned, eventually my emotions would have to line up with my faith. I was trying very hard to maintain the right mental attitude. Every day I battled not to give up or give in to the negative emotions that threatened to overwhelm me. At these low times, one question kept repeating over and over in my mind. *If God is really who He says He is, why am I not seeing the victory in my life?* It became more and more difficult to ignore this line of thinking, and eventually I faced a major crisis of faith.

I shared my concerns with Ken as we had been taught in our counseling sessions. But our framework for dealing with it really hadn't changed. We would pray more and have me pull back from extra responsibilities and take time to rest and regroup. This worked for a while because we had learned to recognize the signs leading to the pit of depression, but eventually we found it was more than the two of us could handle.

When I met Chrystal, we were both young moms and spent a lot of time at church and at women's ministry functions. We became close because our kids were the same age. The Hansen kids spent a lot of time at my home as Chrystal and Ken were super busy being young pastors at a new church. A bond formed between us, and we talked, shared, and mostly laughed all the time about "stuff" in our lives.

The thing I remember that let me know something was changing with Chrystal is when the laughter stopped. She just didn't laugh as easily as we always had. Instead she would cry very easily and not seem to know why. I had no idea that Chrystal's condition was getting as serious as it was until she told me she was seeing a doctor and was "depressed" and would need to slow things down (she led a very busy life). I was good with that until she was suddenly not at church. When she called to tell me that she would have to be totally removed from everything for "a while...with no end date," I understood this was very, very serious.

Chrystal told me that she had to limit contacts and that I was one of a handful of friends that she would see or talk to during this time while she was being treated and "needed to heal." I had no prior knowledge of bipolar disease or mental illness. I knew Chrystal to be strong, smart, and organized. I found it really hard to believe that her mind was not fully functioning. As I would talk to Chrystal over the next few months, a personality change was obvious—she looked like my friend but was not the same person. It hurt deeply.

I was scared to death for her and her beautiful family. As months and months went on, she stopped talking to me. I would get updates on Chrystal through her kids or announcements made to the church. We all prayed and lifted her up to the Lord but wondered if she would ever return to us.[3]

Countdown to a Breakdown

We had three specific incidents happen in our congregation early in 1996 that added even more pressure to my already fragile stability. First, there was the untimely death of one of our church members. Another member was diagnosed with cancer, and then one of the more solid families experienced a very unexpected divorce. As the summer progressed and those incidents occurred one right after another, I began to realize that I had no energy to minister to the needs of these hurting families. It was so overwhelming for me that I couldn't even pretend to pray for them. Defeat grew from the inside out, and I could no longer pretend I had any strength or answers to offer to these families. I was ashamed and embarrassed at my condition, especially because of my position as a leader and minister in the Body of Christ.

Then I started having what's called "detachments of reality," where people would talk to me but I couldn't understand a word they were saying. I knew they were speaking, but it was as if they were speaking a foreign language. The words didn't penetrate into my brain; they floated just outside my ability to comprehend. It was like what they were saying was bouncing right off of me, and I couldn't decipher any of it. It frightened me as I realized that whatever was going on, I had absolutely no control over it.

I ran into my husband's office saying there was something seriously wrong with me. As he held me and quietly talked to me, I began to calm down and we started to rationalize what had just happened to me. It had been a hard four years to start with and then with these three unexpected incidents coming so close together, it was understandable, we reasoned, that it seemed so overwhelming to me. We decided it might help to talk with a counselor who was working in our church building. Ken made an appointment for us for the next day.

The Day

In August 1996, we went to the counselor's office and I tried to explain to him, "I don't know what's wrong with me. I think I'm just too tired." I began crying uncontrollably. It was like we had surgically lanced a boil, and there was this flood of emotion pouring out of me. I was embarrassed by this uncontrollable burst of emotion. I just couldn't hold it in any longer.

The counselor knew immediately what was happening to me. He made a series of phone calls to get me in to see a psychiatrist and receive the right kind of medication and counseling. He knew right away I was having a breakdown and that what I needed was beyond what he could give me. He set up an appointment for me within the next couple of days. But between that day in the counselor's office and the day of my appointment with the psychiatrist, I experienced a total collapse.

The dam had broken, a flood of emotions flooded out of me, and as thoughts of my upcoming appointment with the psychiatrist circled around in my head, I started to hyperventilate. My husband came home to find me curled up in the fetal position, sobbing hysterically in the middle of the kitchen floor. Our children were huddled around me. My seven-year-old son was praying for me; my four-year-old daughter was stroking my hair and telling me everything was going to be alright; while our two-year-old watched.

In talking to my children in retrospect, it seems they did know something was wrong with me but really had no idea what was happening to their mommy. From what my daughter has shared with me, she knew I was sick and tried not to add any more on to me than what was necessary. The two older ones had some sort of sense that if they helped take care of the youngest, then Mommy would get better quicker.

Ryan, now 20 years old, does not specifically recall the day his mom lay crying on the kitchen floor, but he does remember being awakened in the middle of the night by the sounds of an ambulance taking his mother to the hospital. He found some family friends stayed with them as his dad had also gone to the hospital to be with his mom. He was told that everything was alright, but from then on he saw very little of either of his parents. Even when his mom was home he remembers episodes of anger and that she was very moody. They never knew what kind of a mood she would be in so they decided to do as much on their own as they could and not upset her. "I kind of felt like I needed to grow up quickly and sort of fend for myself. I did not want to be a nuisance."

Ryan shares that he saw a "big change, a huge change in his mother's attitude after the healing. …She wasn't moody. It was the total opposite of what she was like before. She seemed real relaxed and a lot of fun. She had lightened up a lot and seemed to be enjoying life."[4]

Reneé, now 18 years old, remembers her mommy being tired and lying on the couch most of the time. "I always wanted to do stuff with her, but she seemed distant and off in her own world somewhere. We realized that Mommy was sick and that we needed to try not to bother her so she could get better. Today we share lots of things together, including a family movie night and try not to allow anything to interfere with it."[5]

Eric remembers coming home from school a couple of times and finding his mom on the floor crying but not really knowing what was going on. "I was in kindergarten or first grade, and my brother and sister would tell me to be good or be quiet and not bother Mommy. I remember it being confusing and not understanding much of what was going on at the time."[6]

I remember going over to their house one time shortly after this. Ken said I could see her so I went in her room. She was in bed, and when I said hi to her, she didn't look my way or even seem to know I was there. It was like looking at a shell of a person who was not connecting with you. It was freaky and not her. It was the difference between Dr. Jekyll and Mr. Hyde. Her hair was all disheveled; she had this blank look of nothingness on her face; and the house was a mess. It was so bizarre seeing her sick like that. I remember that Ken was very distraught and didn't know what was going on with her.[7]

God's Grace for a Season

I was taken to the doctor, given medication, and scheduled to meet regularly with a counselor. All of them were Christians who understood the calling of my life, understood the ministry we were involved in, and understood the Christian walk. They patiently explained that I needed to take the medication because it was God's grace for this season of my life. "If you had heart disease, liver disease, diabetes, lung problems, blood issues, or any other kind of illness, you would take your medication, wouldn't you?" they asked. As I nodded, they went on, "Well, your brain is sick right now and needs medication." I took the medication they prescribed on the basis that it was God's grace for this season.

When Chrystal had her breakdown it was just terrible. She wasn't the Chrystal I knew anymore. She was so sick she couldn't do anything. During her breakdown I was living in New York and she was in Illinois. I knew she was sick and she was different. On the phone she would call sometimes and talk for an hour straight and not make sense. I remember her telling me that she knew how much God loved her and she felt secure in God but everything else didn't make sense. There were times that after I spoke to Chrystal we would call Ken to see how he was doing. She was not functional. She couldn't even dress herself. We met at Ken's parents' house to take the kids to an amusement park one time, and I was shocked when I saw Chrystal. She was so thin and so tired. She wasn't the same happy and chipper Chrystal. She was still sweet but not herself. It was obvious that she was heavily medicated and very ill. Chrystal was totally out of commission.[8]

I am thankful I had good psychiatric care that gave me the right medicine to help my body. I had a Christian counselor who guided me through the mental issues I had suppressed for so long. I had spiritual mentors in my life who understood that my mental illness was rooted in a wounding deep in my spirit.

When God heals and transforms, He is working on the whole man: body, soul, and spirit. We have a physical body; a soul, which is the mind, will, and emotions; and we have a spirit man. What I did not know at the time was that God was healing my body, my soul, and my spirit all at the same time.

My Adventure and Journey With God

1. Read First Thessalonians 5:23. What are the three parts of man that the Bible says need to be dealt with in order to achieve God's peace?

2. Have you ever experienced a "crisis of faith" in your life? If yes, briefly describe it.

3. Can you recall how God was faithful to you in the midst of your situation?

4. Read Psalm 31:22; 34:4-6; 37:1-7. Did David ever doubt that the Lord was there with him in the midst of his trouble? What did David eventually discover about his relationship with God?

5. Pray that the Lord would bring you further revelation concerning your relationship with Him. If you are struggling with seeing God in your struggles, ask a close trusted friend to pray with you. James 5:16 encourages us to confess our hearts and beliefs to one another in order for healing to occur. Sometimes we need to admit our struggles to others and let someone bear our burden. In that act, God ministers and heals our hearts and lives (see Galatians 6:2).

CHAPTER 7

I WANT TO BE NORMAL

I WAS VERY BLESSED to have all Christian doctors. I know that had to be God's design. My psychiatrist and my psychologist both understood my denomination and my role as a pastor's wife, so my beliefs and position were never blamed for my problems. In fact, my doctors were all trying to strengthen my dependence on God in order to bring healing and wholeness. I was at first diagnosed with clinical depression, then bipolar.

Mayo clinic psychiatrist, Daniel K. Hall-Flavin says:

Depression ranges in seriousness from mild, temporary episodes of sadness to severe, persistent depression. Doctors use the term "clinical depression" to describe the more severe, persistent form of depression also known as "major depression" or "major depressive disorder."[1]

Threefold Treatment

The course my doctors prescribed for me included both psychological and chemical treatment. The psychological treatments for clinical depression deal with personality and interpersonal communication. Psychiatric treatments focus on using antidepressants that increase the levels of serotonin, norepinephrine, and dopamine, which are naturally present in the brain, to assist communication between nerve cells.[2]

I would meet once a month with my board-certified psychiatrist, Dr. Kenneth Phillips, to evaluate how I was feeling and to ensure that I was on the right medication. I had to monitor and record my moods four times a day. I had medicine to wake me up in the morning and I had medicine to go to sleep at night. I took medicine for when anxiety hit and medicine if I began moving too fast and my emotions ran too high. I was on nine various prescriptions totaling 1600 milligrams of psychiatric drugs a day.

This sample from my journal shows my moods during this time and reveals just how hard it was becoming for me to handle even the little stresses of everyday life. I was told to use a scale of 1 to 10 with 1 being the worst and 10 being the best.

Monday Morning: 3 (emotional crash)

Evening: 1½ (cried)

Tues. All Day: 2 (adjusting)

Wed. All Day: 2½ (a little better)

Thurs. and Fri.: 3 (pushed myself—couldn't focus—couldn't control—something driving me)

Sat. Morning: 2 (I haven't done anything, feeling anxious)

Evening: 2 (nervous)

Sun. Morning: 3 (anxiety attack at church)

Evening: 2 (Down Day)

Mon. Morning: 1½ (down day—called Dr. Phillips—increased Troz.)

Tues.–Thurs. 1½ to 2 (tired every day—odd—scary—increased Troz. again)

Friday: 2 (Still not able to feel or sense any lift at all, I'm struggling to barely function—something wrong—nervous—jittery)

Dr. Phillips wrote:

> Chrystal Hansen received treatment in our office starting in November of 1996. She initially presented symptoms of depression and anxiety attacks that were severe, and at times incapacitating to her. She also had mood swings and a number of physical symptoms. She was fully cooperative with all of our treatment interventions and received medications as well as regular psychotherapy during this time. Most of her medication was anti-depressant in nature, though she did receive some mood stabilizers. Her recovery was steady but slow.[3]

At one time or another, I was on Lithium, Effexor, Imipramine, Klonopin, and Dexidrine. Medications were the primary way to deal with the physical element of my disease and were used to keep me functioning on a day-to-day basis.

I was connected with a psychotherapist, Trudy Walk. I needed to deal with guilt. I was ashamed that I couldn't be the person I wanted to be. I had to learn how to work through the irrational, emotional outbursts associated with that guilt and shame. I discovered that I was mad at God and my biological father, Carl, for dying. I had a great deal of anger inside my heart.

> My initial session with Chrystal showed she wanted to understand her limits and down areas. Her thinking was dulled, and seemed extra lethargic. She preferred to be out of the house, which caused anxiety as housework accumulated. Dr. Richard Dobbins helped her recognize she was the carrier of her mother's grief. She shared her journal with me, which stated that much of her struggle had to do with loss of control over her time. We talked about changing her life pattern of doing to a slower, less productive pace.[4]

Along with extreme emotional fluctuations, for no apparent reason, my mind would jump from hyper speed to sleep mode. I would have days where I felt I was going to accomplish great things and I would set goals and lay out great plans. The next day I'd wake up at the bottom of the world unable to get out of bed. I found that too many choices, like trying to order off an extensive dinner menu, would trigger a severe anxiety attack.

My psychologist, Trudy Walk, worked to help me bring a measure of balance to this pendulum cycle of thinking and showed me ways to prevent anxiety attacks. She suggested ways to handle things that required making choices or seemed to trigger anxiety attacks. One of the things she suggested was for Ken and I to agree before we went out to dinner that Ken would do the ordering for both of us. I would not even look at the menu. I was to relax and eat whatever was placed in front of me. She helped me to begin to work through one daily activity at a time to try to stabilize each area of daily living.

The Lord added a third dynamic to my treatment regimen. He provided spiritual mentors who helped me understand the anger and hurt that had surfaced toward God. I had to face the fact that I had always thought God was unfair when He took the husband of my 23-year-old pregnant mother. I was very angry that while my father was involved in "Kingdom work" and other people were healed under his ministry, healing never came for him. He had helped so many, yet when he was dying God didn't answer his, my mother's, or my family's prayers. The first thing I had to acknowledge was the anger that existed, and I needed to learn how to deal with it.

Journal Entry 2-20-1998

You have left me with such an incredible hole in my life—one I have wrestled with for as long as I can remember. I'm now almost 35 and still cannot settle the issue. It is such a painful part of me. It has taken all these years to just begin to try and lay it all to rest. It has caused a life of depression, a breakdown, medication, and counseling just to regain any semblance of normal life again. This has pushed me to be an extravert in order to cover the pain, the emptiness, and the insecurity that I have lived with for years, not to mention the anger buried underneath all these layers of living. It has caused embarrassment with family, friends, and my husband. It has caused anger to be poured out on my kids that they don't deserve. God, tell me what I'm supposed to do with all of this garbage? I don't deserve this!

Through my sessions with Trudy Walk, I also discovered I had been trying to protect my mother throughout my life. My mother sat in on one of the sessions with Trudy, and as we talked we discovered there may have been a generational pattern of role reversal, which we discussed more thoroughly at the next session when my mother was with us. Trudy observed, "Chrystal blames herself for 'not loving her (mother) enough.' She feels her mother needed to be affirmed more and Chrystal doesn't feel like she affirmed her enough."[5]

I realize now that God was providing a threefold healing for me using different Christian people, each one trained to deal with a specific aspect of my illness. In order to become whole again, I needed healing in my body, in my soul, and in my spirit.

I have known Chrystal for almost 12 years. My first encounter with Chrystal was actually through a vision. I saw her and another pastor's wife in a hole, and Chrystal had her hand extended upward like she wanted to be pulled out. I remember crying because I could not understand why I was so drawn to her, and I realized I was supposed to pray for her, and I did. I was the children's pastor at that time, and I promised her children that if they ever needed me, I would come. The very first time I went to their home, she was in a fetal position weeping and didn't know who I was. She did allow me to hold her and pray for her until she went to sleep.

I also remember going on a trip with the church, and she was there. I was totally surprised because she wasn't back in church. She kept me and my roommate up until 4:00 in the morning talking non-stop. I felt so honored that she would come to our room to talk since she did not know either of us that well. The one thing she told us was that the doctor had decided to give her shock treatments when she got back home, so we really prayed for her that night. I remember her talking about how difficult it was to dress herself or cook things she had made for years.

One time when Chrystal did come to church, she was very disoriented because of the medication she was on. It gave her the appearance of being intoxicated. During the times that I talked to her after the healing, she talked about her God encounters and how she communicated with Him, and that really amazed me.[6]

Threefold Revelation

The thought that I had been carrying such deep-seated anger against God gave me the first revelation. All my life I had been denying that those feelings were there in my heart. When I acknowledged the fact that I missed my biological father and had always wanted him to be here with me, I was able to truly grieve. With the help of people who understood the hurt and pain in my heart, I was able to go through the grieving process and begin to attain a measure of relief in that area.

Finally being diagnosed with bipolar disorder gave me another interesting revelation. It seems my brain was missing a crucial transmitter or stabilizing bar. From what the science realm tells us, this is an inherited condition due to a gene dispensation.[7] In discussing my ancestry, I learned that my maternal grandmother had lived with the struggles of mental illness. That was in the 1940s and '50s when they didn't have the understanding we do today.

Back then, families of the mentally ill had basically two "treatment" choices: either put their loved one away in an insane asylum or learn to live with the condition with relatively little medical or psychological help. I don't have many memories of my maternal grandmother. She died when I was four, but my mother told me about her. They never put her away, but my mother remembered there was a lot of mental anguish and struggle in her life. My mother always felt she needed to take care of her mother.

I remember a time when I realized my daughter was assuming a similar mind-set of wanting to "take care of Mommy." Reneé was around six years old, and I had experienced a particularly bad anxiety attack. Ken came home and calmed me down. I guess I wasn't really aware of the fact that Ryan and Reneé were witnessing the whole thing. Shortly after that it was time for the kids to go to bed. Reneé turned to me and said, "Mommy, if you need me tonight, wake me up and I'll come pray for you again." I was shocked as I saw how my little daughter was taking on the role of the parent, trying to protect me and pray for me until I could get better.

When I ask Reneé now what she remembers about my illness, she says she remembers the box of pills on top of the microwave and wondering if Mommy was ever going to get well again. (We had decided to put all of my pills in a bright green box—out in plain sight but out of the reach of little hands—so I would remember to take them. We didn't realize they were a constant reminder to our children that Mommy was very sick.)

Another Discouraging Revelation

With the bipolar diagnosis came the revelation that there was a physical lack that was causing part of the problem. Along with that knowledge came another rather discouraging revelation. My doctor said, "Outside of a miracle from God, Chrystal, you're going to have to learn to live with this. We can medicate it and you can live a fairly normal life, but you're going to have to learn how to maneuver through this because you're actually missing this component in your brain that stabilizes your moods."

My depression symptoms seemed to increase during certain months of the year so I needed ways to overcome this seasonal depression cycle.

January and February seemed to be particularly difficult months. In one of our January counseling session notes, Trudy Walk wrote:

> Chrystal was tearful and anxious and not sleeping at night due to body tenseness. January and February are depressing months. I needed to remind her that being depressed was not her fault. Chrystal said she did not like being depressed because it sets her apart from others.[8]

And my friend Stacey Brown wrote:

> I was a church leader and personal friend during the time of Chrystal's illness. When I first met Chrystal I was amazed at the amount of energy she always seemed to have. Her oldest child was the same age as my youngest child and although we are two years apart in age, she ran circles around me. I had no idea at the time that this behavior was part of her "manic" cycles. She continued to be a great teacher and leader for the women's group. The first signs that something was amiss occurred when we saw her energy levels plummet. It appeared to be seasonal at first, but then it caused her to pull back from more and more things. She basically dropped out of sight for a while, but Pastor Ken explained that we needed to give her time to heal and so we backed off and gave her space. We took the kids on play dates to give Chrystal some time alone to heal and we prayed for her full recovery.[9]

Even with revelation in those two areas of my life, I still did not experience any real peace or normality. Ken and I knew that God hadn't brought us this far to have us coast through the rest of our lives barely able to keep things on an even keel. We were dealing with the grief I had suppressed all my life, and now we knew there was a physical cause for the mood swings. We both felt there was a third aspect of my healing that was still missing. We asked God to bring us revelation, and He answered that prayer.

I Do Know I Love Horses

One day as Ken and I sat in the car overlooking a forest preserve in our city and feeling totally confounded by the whole situation, a woman came by riding a horse on the trail in front of us. I said to my husband, "I don't know who I am or who I will be. I don't have any idea how this is all going to turn out, but I do know that I love horses." In that moment my husband grabbed hold of that one insight and said, "Let's believe and agree together that God will bring the opportunity for you to ride again."

As we moved into the fall of 1996, we connected with a family in our church who owned horses, and I began to ride on a regular basis. At times it was very, very difficult to go, but I would force myself. When I was on the back of a horse, whether we were on a trail or walking country roads, peace would fill my spirit. I could hear and sense the comfort of the Lord, and at least on the back of a horse, I would feel a little normal.

Some of the most beautiful times during that painful season in my life were spent on horseback, enjoying nature. Whether it was a springtime ride enjoying the newly budded flowers and trees or a chilly ride on a snowy winter day, returning to riding helped me connect and regain some of my self-image. I was a bit apprehensive at first, but my childhood love for horses prevailed. It took me a while to regain my confidence, but I soon fell in love with one of my friend Linda's horses named Amber Bar. She had been with Linda for many years and was a spunky older quarter horse, reliable and dependable, while still lively and fun to ride.

Linda and I arranged to ride together every Monday when Ken was off and could watch the kids. This enabled me to give myself most of the day to be with a wonderful friend and her horses. Riding became therapy for me. Once there I found rest and peace returning as we rode. Linda became a wonderful confidant during that time. I could share my heart with her and knew I was safe in her presence.

At first Chrystal was a little uncomfortable and needed to be reminded of certain things like cinching the saddle and cleaning the horse's hooves. But after I showed her something once, she was able to remember and do it fine. When she came the first time she was quite nervous, timid, and sad and seemed to me very thin. There were times she would come and park her car at the stables and just go in to the barn and sit and cry. For about two or three weeks we tried different horses for her until she fell in love with my daughter's horse. Once Chrystal and the horse bonded, it was much more relaxing for her, and her confidence started coming back.[10]

Our riding together lasted through the entire illness and continued until I began regaining my life and responsibilities back. Amber Bar was aging, and our time together slowly dwindled away. I was so thankful for what God had done during that battle and how loving He was to reconnect me with a childhood pleasure. Linda and I have often talked and reminisced about those rides and hoped that one day we would return to riding together. Looking back, I see that God showed up whenever I needed Him, though I was not aware of it at the time. He had set in place the treatment I needed in all three areas of my life. We were not to see the full impact of this for several more years.

The Medicine Isn't Working

For three years, my family lived daily in an atmosphere where I struggled mentally and emotionally. Not only was I not there for them, they often had to be there for me. The treatment period of antidepressant drugs, psychiatric drugs, and the counseling did give me the feeling that I was gaining an understanding as to why I had been depressed as a child. I grieved the loss of my father, so some of the things I had been dealing with were getting better. The realization that living with bipolar disease was going to be a lifelong struggle set in. Was I going to be like this the rest of my life?

> Once Chrystal was placed on medication she returned to attending church more often. However, it really wasn't Chrystal! She was a shell of her former self. Chrystal got better at going through the motions, but there was no real life behind her words; and when not specifically being addressed, she would just stare. She became more physically functional, without engaging mentally or emotionally. Over time we saw Chrystal "return" a little more emotionally. We were never really sure how big of a factor the medications were in her detachment. One of the more devastating parts of her final diagnosis was that Chrystal would have to remain on medications for the rest of her life. This meant to us that we would never fully get Chrystal back, that she would continue to "hold us at arm's length" emotionally. Her spark and spunk were gone...forever![11]

Not only were they telling me I would have to be on medication for the rest of my life, I started experiencing some side effects from all the medication I was taking. I had been told that most of the psychiatric medication I would be taking had a tendency to cause weight gain. Not just a few pounds here and there but an exorbitant amount of weight. For whatever reason, the medication had an opposite effect on me. It sped up my metabolism so much that I couldn't keep weight on. I was almost anorexic, dropping down to 110 pounds.

Everyone worried over the fact that I had no appetite and continued to lose weight. Part of the problem was that I couldn't remember if I had eaten anything. My husband would come home from work and ask me if I'd eaten and I didn't know if I had or not. I could not retain information, so unless someone sat right there with me and watched me eat, we had no idea how much food I was actually consuming in a day.

We met over 28 years ago at youth camp where we were the speakers and the worship team. Ken and Chrystal brought their youth group. I remember Ken talking with me after an amazing service. We all became friends and we have been on mission trips with them a number of times to England and Portugal. A number of years into our relationship we noticed that Chrystal was getting more withdrawn and not as open and receptive to us as she used to be. We could tell she was avoiding us when we were at the church. At the house we noticed she was having a hard time putting things in order, and tasks that were easy before seemed difficult.

One time we were at their home and the kids had learned to tell when an episode was coming on their mom and they said, "Mom—don't give in to the dark side." That was a defining moment for us in realizing how serious this was. Then Ken told us about Chrystal seeing the therapist and about her sickness and that she was on a lot of meds.

Ken came to our headquarters in Indianapolis about once a month when he could to get away, talk, rest, and think. We felt his pain and aloneness through this time as he was now responsible for raising the children, doing all the household work, and pastoring the church. He loved Chrystal deeply but was at a total loss about what to do. This went on for so long, and our hearts hurt for both of them as they wrestled through this.[12]

Psychotic Episodes

I began experiencing frequent psychotic episodes (also known as "brief reactive psychosis"), which is basically a short-term break from reality. These episodes can include delusions, hallucinations, and disorganized speech and behavior.[13] I could not determine what was real and what wasn't.

I began to understand the fear and the danger of these psychotic episodes. What if I chose to believe that the unreal was real? Would I step over the line and never come back to reality? I had several incidents where I had trouble choosing whether something was really happening or not, and each time it became more and more frightening.

I remember one incident that happened while I was staying at a friend's house for a weekend of counseling. I woke up in the middle of the night and went to the top of the stairs. I looked down the stairs and saw a light and heard voices. My first thought was that my friends must have gotten up and were down there talking for some reason. But then I saw that their bedroom door was closed and realized that if the door was closed it meant they were sleeping. But then I began to waver, are they sleeping or are they downstairs where the light and voices are coming from? The question kept circling in my head, yet I could not find an answer. Why couldn't I figure this out?

Then I thought, *It's the middle of the night, it's dark, of course they are sleeping.* Then I started wondering, *Is it the middle of the night or is it the middle of the day?* I could not determine whether it was day or night. *What if I make the wrong choice? What will happen if I choose to go down the stairs and what I see is not really there? Should I knock on their door? What if it's the middle of the day and I choose to believe it's the middle of the night?* I couldn't even decide what to decide. All I could do in that moment of utter confusion was cry out to God. "Dear God, I don't know what to do. I am going to lose my mind."

Even through all of the confusion, I sensed the Lord saying, "If you lose your mind, you won't lose Me."

I had been living for months with the overwhelming fear that one of these times I would choose wrong and would lose my ability to chose Christ. And if I lost this cognitive ability to chose I would perhaps go straight to hell. When the Lord told me that even if I lost my mind, I wouldn't lose Him, I went back to bed and slept through the night. When I woke the next morning, I told my friends what had happened and they said they had not gotten up or gone downstairs; they were asleep all night.

> Chrystal is experiencing manic cycling on a daily basis. She is not able to sleep well at night. Talked about her last visit with Dr. Phillips where she failed to talk about her grief response to her grandmother's recent death which may be contributing to her increased sleeping (during the day), her grief and increased reliance on meds.[14]

Another summer began and I found myself getting more and more frustrated that there did not seem to be any real progress toward what I considered normal life. One day I cried out, "Lord, the medicine isn't working. My doctors are frustrated and I'm not getting any better. Is this the way I have to live for the rest of my life?"

I was continually in counseling and talking with my doctor concerning other options to consider since I seemed to be at a standstill. One option was to go to see other doctors in the city who were more proficient in dealing with severe cases of bipolar like mine. Another option that had been used on others with severe symptoms such as mine was shock therapy. Open to just about anything at this point, I asked what shock therapy was and how it worked.

Electroconvulsive therapy (ECT), also known as electroshock, is a controversial psychiatric treatment in which seizures are electrically induced in anesthetized patients for therapeutic effect. Today, ECT is most often used as a treatment for severely depressed patients who have not responded to other treatment and is also used in the treatment of mania (often in bipolar disorder), catatonia, schizophrenia, and other disorders.[15]

Apparently, it wouldn't eliminate the bipolar condition, but somehow it would either numb or stabilize the brain better than the medication could by itself. The doctor told us that ECT had been a relatively effective treatment for severe depression and in some cases did appear to improve the quality of life in both short- and long-term patients. However, drug therapy would probably still need to be continued. At the time there was controversy over whether ECT caused permanent memory loss and possible brain damage. Since that time the American Psychiatric Association and the British National Institute for Health and Clinical Excellence have concluded that the procedure does not cause brain damage in adults.[16]

I spoke with Ken after the doctor had talked to them about the possibility of shock therapy. When I asked him how things were going with Chrystal, he looked at me with a look of utter despair and said, "They're thinking of doing shock therapy! We just don't know what to do!" I remember thinking; this is really serious for them to be considering shock therapy on her. I hadn't seen Chrystal in about six months when she came to an event at the church. She looked unhealthy and thin. She stood in the lobby against the wall and looked like she was watching a TV program that she was in no way involved in. If anyone tried to talk to her, she would try to engage in the conversation but had a blank look on her face most of the time. Everyone was trying to be very careful around her but she still disappeared for a while for a "breather."[17]

A Chapter Closed

In April 1998, I received a call that my paternal grandmother was not expected to live through the week. I told Ken I needed him to go with me, and he was very supportive through my grandmother's death and funeral.

Journal entry—April 9, 1998

April 9th, 1998, was a day I never wanted to come. Grandma died at 1:00 P.M. this afternoon. I feel this was the last tie to Carl—but Ken has encouraged me that it is only the beginning to an open door to speak freely of what is in my heart concerning Carl. Grandma had often said that she was looking forward to seeing Carl—it had been 35 years since his death. I can hear her saying, "Oh, Chrissy," the phrase she used every time I came to visit or talk on the phone. She was such an encouraging lady, who lived by the verse, "this is the day the Lord has made, I will rejoice and be glad." I have wonderful memories of her as a child, teen, and adult. She truly had an impact on molding my life.

The feeling surrounding my grandmother's death was great sadness because she was so dear to me. She was the most loving and caring person I knew, always encouraging and always praying for me. It was the end of a major connection with Carl, and yet little did I know that her death was timed to be part of my healing and my new life.

Journal entry—April 15, 1998

It's April 15ᵗʰ, 1998, and I'm sitting at the grave sites of my grandparents and Carl. I've arranged the flowers for all three graves. I've cried some, but where do I go from here? Maybe nowhere. Carl William Hahn—I know him in name only, not as a person. I don't seem to be grieving for my grandmother as much as I thought I would. My grief and pain is directed at Carl. Grandpa and Grandma had reasons to go home, old age and sickness, but Carl, seems such an injustice. I've asked the Lord what He wants to say to me—and my soul is quieted and still.

Carl, I know you by name only, but how I wish I could have known you in person.

Journal entry—April 16, 1998

Today, April 16, 1998, my mother and I went to visit my grandparents' and Carl's grave one more time before I left for home. It was hard, but I really didn't cry too much. We visited other family members' graves, my mom's mother and great grandparents. Then off to my grandmother's house. So much has already changed that it wasn't Grandma's home anymore. I walked the grounds for one last time, remembering where the trees and shrubs used to be. What a flood of memories returned. But all is changed, and this chapter of my life has started to close. Oh, how I wish it wouldn't.

After coming home from my grandmother's funeral, I was given a new journal as a gift. I wrote the following in my journal on April 17ᵗʰ, 1998.

Journal entry—April 17, 1998

I choose today to begin this new journal. My grandmother died on April 9ᵗʰ of last week. The print on this journal is entitled, "The Garden of Prayer" by Thomas Kinkade. It summarizes her life. I can barely keep my eyes off it. It causes me to remember the anthem of her life—prayer! There is a path in the picture that leads through the garden and at the end of that path stands a woman; this is even significant because Grandma had a prayer path through their woods that she walked frequently. I remember walking that path with her on many occasions. I can't express what I feel, but something has come to life in me and given me direction.

Something happened once my grandmother passed. I was forced to bring closure to this chapter of my life and yet sensed a new one would begin. I had no idea of what that looked like, only a spark of hope and a measure of determination that God was doing something in me.

I Just Want to Be Normal

In July 1998, I was given an extremely addictive prescription that I was only allowed to be on for two weeks. There were two reasons I wanted to take this drug. It was a safer type of stimulant than the ECT procedure, and I really wanted to go to the "Awake America Crusade" being held in Iowa. I needed to be with normal people, try to stay overnight in a fairly protected environment, and attend an uplifting Christian conference. I hadn't been able to do any of those things for such a long time. My heart hungered for even a small oasis of normality even if it was only temporary. I hoped by carefully regulating my activities and taking the strong prescription I could at least manage enough to go to the conference with a group of caring people from our church.

I just wanted to be normal. I just wanted to be like everybody else. As we walked out the door to head for the conference, I prayed, "Lord, You've got to get this medication to work if only just for this conference. I want to worship and praise You and give You honor but I can't if this medicine doesn't work!"

My Adventure and Journey With God

1. What are the three tools that God used to bring about healing in me? If after reading this chapter, you sense that you have experienced some of these same feelings and emotions in your life, but have not sought the help of professionals, now is the time. It is important to be under good Christian counseling during cycles of depression that interrupt your daily routine of living. Please speak with your pastor or a trusted friend and seek professional help.

2. If you or a family member is presently experiencing or diagnosed with a similar condition, are you being cared for properly? Are the body, soul, and spirit being ministered to effectively? And do you have family supports? (If yes, rejoice and continue in your care staying faithful to the course you are on. If no, ask the Lord to show you your next step and consult pastoral or spiritual counsel.)

3. Have you ever experienced a chapter closing in your life? What was happening? And what do you believe God was doing?

4. As you have read from my journals some of the most difficult times of my life, what are your thoughts? Do you feel

encouraged in your spirit, inspired to journal, or amazed to see God use such difficult situations for good?

5. Journaling has many benefits. Sadly many do not enter into this experience due to intimidation or lack of seeing the benefit. May I share a few of the benefits of this exercise with you. First, journaling brings a tangible focus to your thoughts and feelings. It also helps to open areas of your heart that otherwise might go undetected. And it provides opportunities for deeper reflection as you look at the words on paper rather than just thinking of the feelings or emotions. I would encourage you to begin small. Buy a special notebook and start writing about Scripture verses and how they minister to you. Or write out your questions to God, listening for His quiet voice in return. Or begin to write about a feeling or thought in letter form to the Lord. Just begin; there is no right or wrong in journaling. It's how you would want to express and write.

CHAPTER 8

A WHOLE NEW MIND

I DID GO TO THE CONFERENCE and made it all the way through to the last night. It was wonderful! I carefully navigated myself through each day, resting when I needed to rest, and pacing myself carefully so as not to trigger either a high or a low episode. I was also prescribed a medication to help with keeping my energy levels higher so I could manage the trip. It appeared the Lord was answering my prayer and I was really enjoying the gift He had given me.

Life Changing

It was the last meeting of the conference and was being held in a huge arena. I suddenly felt an overwhelming urge to move away from where our church group was sitting. I felt like God was saying, "Come on over here, worship where it is just you and Me." I had just recently been able to start to worship again, so I went and stood by the railing within sight of my husband but away from the group. The very first song that night was, "The Enemy Is Under My Feet." The Lord said, "Just remember that, he's under your feet." As I gave myself to that time of worship, the Lord began to do a work in me that I really can't put into words. I don't remember what the rest of the songs were, I just remember talking to the Lord from that moment on about all the struggles that I was facing and everything else that had led up to that moment in time.

During those 40 minutes of worship, the Lord began to deal with one area at a time, like peeling back an onion. I remember how vivid and clear He spoke to me. In my mind's eye, I saw a large stone blocking my steps and fences lined up in front of me. I could not get around the stone and I heard the Lord say, "Just step on it," and as I did I then heard, "Don't look back." He led me to forgive one person and deal with several other things I needed to confess. Each time I obeyed, a fence would fall and the Lord would instruct me to stand on it and not look back.

At one point, He began to guide me through what I would later discover is the breaking of generational curses. I got to the last fence and the Lord brought a memory back regarding a great-grandmother who was involved with spiritualism. Suddenly I thought about two things that had happened just before we left for the conference. First, a very trustworthy confidant who had been faithfully praying for us told me he felt the Lord would deal with a specific spiritual issue in my life. He told me that he felt I had been very faithful to follow my doctors' orders and had done all that was required of me in the physical realm. Now God was going to take it into the spiritual realm and do what only He could do.

The second thing I remember came from a conversation with my mom just before we had left. My mom and dad came to watch the kids for us while we were at the conference. My mother asked me for a photo of her mother that I had gotten reproduced for her. I went to a photo album, and as I was flipping through, there was a picture of a woman my grandmother had lived with and embraced as a "grandmother" in her life. Out of the blue, mother stopped me and asked, "Do you know who that is?" I answered that it was my grandma's grandmother. She nodded and said, "Did you know she was involved in some form of spiritualism?" Apparently she participated in séances, speaking with spirits, and embracing spiritual guides. I recalled hearing that story before but thought it was odd that it resurfaced now. I placed it in the back of my mind as we headed for the conference.

At the conference, the Lord reminded me of that conversation and said, "That's the spiritual matter I'm going to contend with." I reminded the Lord that I had gone through "Bondage Breakers" and broken off curses from my past. The Lord said, "You did not break it off in connection with the mental illness." I immediately prayed, "If there is any connection of this mental illness to what this woman was involved in—the witchcraft, the occult, or whatever she dabbled in—Lord, I don't want any of that."

In that moment I sensed something coming out of the left side of my head, like a little drawer handle. When I asked God what was happening, He said, "Pull it out and throw it on the ground." As I started physically going through the motions, I heard the Lord say, "You don't need your medicine anymore."

Oh, no, no, no, no, I can't, I thought, pulling my hand back from the handle. I had been told I would need to take the medicine forever. If I ever started to feel better and got to the point I felt I could go without medicine, I needed to go back to my doctors before changing any of the doses. They had warned me that they would have to bring me down slowly because stopping my medicine cold turkey was very dangerous. I had been very faithful about following those directions. In this moment, I knew that if I was not hearing the Lord correctly, I could permanently damage myself and perhaps never get well enough to function again.

I argued this point with the Lord for several minutes, even offering to go off slowly and visit my doctors so they could monitor the decrease of medication, but the Lord would not agree to that. Finally, I had to either walk away from the moment or trust that I was hearing His voice. The problem I had in making that decision was the fear that I was in one of those moments of detachment from reality.

Yet something had happened when I said that simple prayer about denouncing anything that had come down that generational line. There was definitely something different inside my mind. I said, "All right, Lord, I'm going to trust You. I'm going to believe that I can walk away from this medication." I grabbed the handle and threw it down three times. As soon as I came into agreement with the Lord, it was as if a light switch went on and I regained my whole mind in that moment. There was suddenly a clarity I had never experienced before. I stood there with my eyes closed, stunned by what I was experiencing.

Trying to fully grasp what had just happened, I began to have the most amazing vision.

Standing in a place I have never dreamed nor seen before; a high place on a balcony overlooking a vast and spacious place. The colors were the most magnificent shades of midnight blues, with the clearest of white stars scattering the sky. And shades of yellow and white light lined the horizon against a dark midnight blue. The air was crisp, clean, and cool yet so very still. A sense of awe was definitely present and to breathe seemed to be disrespectful, yet to fill your lungs with the biggest sigh was exhilarating. To move seemed impossible, yet my eyes were drawn from horizon to horizon and back again, trying to take in the essence of this place. However I was not able to even grasp an ounce. (Taken from my journal dated July 21, 1998.)

I immediately realized I had never had a whole mind; there had always been something lacking. I knew without a shadow of a doubt that God had just healed me. I kicked into my religious mind-set and asked, "What do I do now, Lord?" I'd seen people who were healed run to the platform and scream, "I'm healed! I'm healed!" I knew if I did that, my husband and church family would try and explain it away since I was technically mentally ill. So I was completely left dumbfounded as to what to do. I felt the Lord tell me to go back to my seat and quietly sit down. No one had prayed for me; there was no prophetic call from the platform saying this is happening in the audience; it just was me and God.

I went and sat down next to my husband; I wanted to tell him what had just happened to me. I thought to myself, *He needs to know about this,* but at the same time I felt like the Lord led me to the Scripture verse where the angel appeared to Mary telling her she would be the Lord's mother. Instead of running out into the street and proclaiming it to the world, she pondered those things in her heart. The Lord said, "That's all I want you to do. Don't say a word to anyone; just ponder it in your heart." I had trusted God this far, so I went 24 hours without saying anything to my husband. I did not take any medicine the rest of that day. A sort of calm serenity washed over me and I just relaxed and enjoyed what God was doing as I pondered all that had happened in my heart.

I was with Ken and Chrystal on the trip to Iowa where she was miraculously healed. Several amazing things took place during that weekend, and many from our church were touched by God. We were all praying that Chrystal would be one of the people healed. When Chrystal began to share that God had healed her, I was excited and scared because I had witnessed many people "flipping out" who had gone off of their medications because they thought they no longer needed to be medicated. But as I sat with her and heard her talk, I realized that this was different. She was sharing from her heart, not just giving perfunctory answers. She also was willing to contact her physicians regarding her healing and follow their lead concerning the medications. This thrilled me! If she was willing to do all this "under a microscope," then indeed God had healed her! We laughed and cried tears of joy together. We had an amazing time together, and I'd gotten my friend back![1]

When we got home from the conference the next day, I fell asleep on the couch—which was nothing unusual. When I woke up I thought I was experiencing a psychotic episode—like I might have dreamed everything that happened at the conference. I started to panic, fearing I really messed myself up by not taking medication for 24 hours. I then heard the Lord say, "Go tell your husband what happened."

I went upstairs and said to Ken, "I believe I was healed at the conference." Then I told him the whole story, including the fact that I had not taken any medication for the last 24 hours.

Ken knew I had reached a point where I could not go even one hour without medication. If I missed a scheduled dose I would either hit the ceiling or crash on the floor. He just looked at me and said, "You really haven't had any medicine for 24 hours?" When I nodded yes, he declared,

"You're healed!" When he validated the healing, something solidified in me that *Yes, I was healed.* When I woke up from my nap questioning reality, it was the enemy attempting to take away my healing.

When Ken prayed with me that night, I went to sleep immediately, which was highly unusual. I've not taken any medicine since that day.

I Know What a Whole Mind Is

I woke up the next morning with such clarity of mind, that I told Ken, "Now I know what a whole mind is. I've never had a whole mind before, but now I do!" It was like all my life there had been a roadblock in my thought process. I had struggled with unstable emotions and wavered in my faith. During the illness, I had experienced a severe inability to do even simple things that I wanted to do because I couldn't think through the necessary process. All of a sudden, it was as if every pathway in my brain was clear and it was working.

I guess it would be like being born with a limp arm, thinking that was "normal" and living with it all your life. You would not know what it is to have two working arms until that arm suddenly functioned properly. That's how it was with my thought process. I didn't realize I had an impaired thought process. When my mind was made whole, I realized, "Oh, that's how it's supposed to work!" Mentally, I was doing great, but now I had to bring the physical realm into agreement with what had happened to me at the conference.

When I started working for Chrystal as her part-time assistant in June of 2006, I did not know all that she had gone through. To find out what she went through and see what she does today, you see one of God's wonderful miracles! What amazes me most about her is her ability to use both the right and the left sides of her brain. To be honest, I can never remember which side of the brain controls what, let alone be able to use both sides! She is a very creative person, but unlike many creative people I've met, she can focus on many other details and many other tasks. She has so much going on that I don't know how she keeps up with everything. I'm a detail-oriented person and she makes my eyeballs spin.[2]

Physical Alignment

My psychiatrist and my psychologist were both very upset when I told them I had stopped taking all of my medication. They knew that normally when you suddenly stop taking this type of medication you are likely to go through major withdrawal.

Chrystal described a religious experience this week at the "Awake America" conference. She described it as God having her "step on a stone" and when she did various fences were knocked over: anger, depression, bipolar, and medication. She has stopped her meds and is feeling fine. She seemed excited and energetic but no feelings of mania.[3]

Mentally I was fine, but physically I did go through symptoms of drug withdrawal. It was horrible and a little confusing to me. "God," I said, "You healed my mind, why is my body shaking so badly?"

Ken remembers the difficult days when Chrystal was going through the physical withdrawal from the medication. "I was afraid she was getting worse instead of better, but she kept saying that mentally she was all right. I was amazed at her clarity in spite of the physical symptoms. It took ten days for the physical withdrawal symptoms to run their course, and then it was all over. It was like a switch had been flipped on and my wife was back!"

God sent a dear friend to me to help me understand what I was going through. We went to the story in the Bible where Jesus cursed the fig tree that was not bearing fruit (see Mark 11:12-24). That tree did not die immediately when Jesus said those words. It was the next morning as the disciples passed by the fig tree they noticed it had withered from the roots up. It took time for what was spoken in the spiritual realm to manifest in the physical realm. They assured me, "What you received in the spiritual realm was truth. You are healed. It will come to the physical realm as you continue to believe what you experienced spiritually."

So I got up each morning, looked at myself in the mirror, and prayed, "I thank You, Lord, for my healing; just bring my body into alignment."

I shared the story of what happened to me at the conference with my psychiatrist. He said, "Chrystal, I do believe you are healed. We'll just monitor this over the next few months and help you in any way we can to move forward with your life." He actually validated the fact that what I experienced was indeed God.

Ken admits it took some getting used to. "I would wake up at night and just look at her. I had lived with the dysfunction of her illness for so long I kept wondering when the other shoe would drop. It was such a dramatic thing that God did that I have to admit it took a while for my brain to be able to wrap around it. We decided to watch her closely for the next month and then tell our church family what God had done."

"Chrystal is doing well. She feels like God gave her a new mind. She is sleeping well, waking at 7:00 A.M. and beginning her day with energy and hope," Trudy Walk wrote in her counseling notes one month after Chrystal's healing experience.[4]

Ken remembers the day they told their loving congregation what had happened:

> When we stood up together and told our church family what God had done for us at the *Awake America* conference, it set off a wave of faith like we had not witnessed in our church in the six years we had been there. For the next three years our church grew by leaps and bounds. We were seeing a harvest after all the seed we had sown. People had faith to believe for so many things because of what God did in Chrystal's life.

I continued to see all of my doctors for a year after that day. I wanted them to verify my healing. I valued the care my doctors had given me and wanted them to release me when they were comfortable saying, "Chrystal, you're fine; there's nothing else we can do." My medical records confirm both the diagnosis and the healing. I carry with me today a letter from my psychiatrist stating the reality of the healing I received from the Lord.[5] I took 1600 milligrams of drugs going into that conference and have never had a drug since then. I am a living testimony of our miracle-working God.

> When I saw Chrystal after her miraculous healing, the difference was like night and day. My first thoughts when I heard about the healing were, I believe in healing and all but she was bipolar and on lots of medication. But when I saw her it was like a light bulb had gone on; the brightness had returned in her face. Even in the first week or two she was talking and communicating but not like when she was manic. There was definitely a big difference. We had conversations of her healing where she openly and honestly talked about stopping her medicine. She was honest and coherent. She was very balanced, excited but not hyper. The brightness had come back and she was alive again.[6]

Journey Into Wholeness

Ken and Chrystal's marriage is blessed by God! Their family, too. They've endured so much and have come out on the other side—I believe better. There is hope and freedom on the other side of adversity. When Chrystal received her healing it was definitely evident. It was miraculous! She called me and told me when God healed her and how she went to her doctors and went off of her meds cold turkey—which is not recommended—but Chrystal felt certain that was the way God wanted her to do it. Chrystal's life was transformed when she was healed, when God *totally* healed her. She no longer had any signs of depression. After the healing, Chrystal took it slowly, gradually adding things to her life and while still seeing her doctors. It was so cute because several years ago Chrystal said she made a cassette tape about her illness to help others. I believe she named it, "Coming out of the Blues." When she told us the title we were all (Ken, Chrystal, myself, and my husband, Dwayne) standing in their kitchen and I just busted out laughing! I said, "Oh my goodness, Chrystal, you were much more than blue when you were sick! You were *crazy!*" I can tell her that because she's healed now and I'm one of her best friends! My point is that even after she came out of the illness, she still didn't realize just how sick she had been. Chrystal is one of the best friends I've had and ever will have. We've been through a lot together. We've shared the good and bad in our lives. Our families are close and will forever be.[7]

Our journey into wholeness is a lifelong adventure with God. Philippians 1:6 says:

And I am convinced and sure of this very thing, that He Who began a good work in you will continue until the day of Jesus Christ [right up to the time of His return], developing [that good work] and perfecting and bringing it to full completion in you (Philippians 1:6 AMP).

God desires to bring us through all of our circumstances, trials, and tribulations into a place of wholeness. However, we will find that this is a lot easier said than done. If we try to do it in our own strength and in our own way, it will appear to be impossible. But we know and must live like we believe that *"with God all things are possible"* (Matt. 19:26; see also Mark 10:27; Luke 18:27). Our part is to learn to respond to what God is doing in us and place ourselves where God can best work in us.

Coming into wholeness starts by asking, "God, what are You doing here in this place?" Then we must learn to respond to what He is saying. Each of our journeys will be different. No two are ever the same. There are no quick fixes or "exit here" signs along the way. There are only paths to follow and three important truths that we must allow to penetrate our hearts and renew our minds. Our security, our significance, and our freedom are all in Christ.

Renewing Our Minds

Part of my healing process came when God told me He would still love me even if I couldn't love Him. He also assured me that if I lost my mind, I would not lose Him. These two assurances from God helped me begin to move away from the performance mentality I had developed throughout my life. To change a lifelong mind-set, we must follow Romans 12:2: *"Do not conform any longer to the pattern of this world, but be transformed by the renewing of your mind."* Renewing the mind does not come naturally; there is no automatic "delete button" that erases all the bad information and programming we have received. We have to surrender our human understanding and embrace who we are from God's perspective.

The most important belief we possess is truly knowing who God is. The second most important belief is who we are as children of God. It is not what we do that determines who we are. It is who we believe we are that determines what we will do. We have been fully accepted into Christ as a child of the Most High God. This right was given to us by God the Father. We are not brought into salvation by how we behave, but how we believe.

> *Yet to all who received Him, to those who believed in His name, He gave the right to become children of God—children born not of natural descent, nor of human decision or a husband's will, but born of God* (John 1:12-13).

If you have read this story of God's love and miraculous healing power and have never personally invited Christ to be a part of your life's journey, I encourage you to simply ask Him now. He is waiting for your invitation. Simply pray, "Lord Jesus, I recognize I have lived my life without You and I desperately need You to be with me. I invite You into my life's journey, to guide me, to teach me, to heal me, and to forgive me of my sins. I don't want to travel alone anymore. Come into my heart and life today. Amen."

Security in Christ

When people are anxious, it is usually because they do not know what is going to happen, giving them a sense of uncertainty and insecurity. My insecurities stemmed from losing my biological father before I was born. Then these deep insecurities surfaced when I entered into a marriage relationship with Ken. I fluctuated between bouts of jealousy and rage fed by my fear of losing him like I did my father. I was looking for security in the wrong places.

Some of us look for security in physical places. Others look for their sense of security in their financial holdings; still many look for a sense of security in temporal relationships. If we put too much stock in our earthly relationships and surroundings, they may subtly replace God as the significant other in our lives. Paul warns us about trying to find our approval from men rather than from God. Galatians 1:10 says, *"Am I now trying to win the approval of men, or of God? Or am I trying to please men? If I were still trying to please men, I would not be a servant of Christ."*

Significance in Christ

Levels of employment and the number of degrees we have are viewed with great significance in our society. We often measure our significance by how much money we have accrued or the titles after our names. We honor those who have accomplished much in their professions, those who are entrepreneurs or have served the common good in our society. Great value is extended toward those whose contributions have led to the betterment of mankind. Yet much of what is valued in this life is not of eternal value, thus it profits us nothing and often causes great stress within us as we strive to achieve significance.

I lived on a self-imposed pedestal with the title of superwoman stamped under my name. I strove to excel at whatever I was doing, hoping to earn a place of significance in the eyes of men and of God. The truth I was missing was that my title was *"child of God and co-heir with Christ"* (see Rom. 8:17). I had been called by God to be His child.

Yes, I was called to please Him, but His love for me was not given based on my achievements.

As a matter of fact, the Word says He loved me and sent His Son Jesus to die for me while I was still a mixed-up, confused sinner (see Rom. 5:8). We can be raised as a Christian and grow up in church and still not truly understand how significant we are to the Father. I felt God wasn't answering my prayers the way I thought He should because I was still insignificant in His eyes. The truth is that He formed me in my mother's womb and He made me so unique that there is not another one of His children just like me (see Ps. 139:13-17).

Part of my dilemma was caused by comparing myself to other Christians and thinking they were God's favorites because He seemed to answer their prayers and didn't answer mine. Most of my friends in school lived with their two biological parents while God had chosen to take one of mine to Heaven right before I was born. I watched as others in our church were healed of all kinds of sickness and yet I continued to struggle with an internal unrest and pain. By comparing my situation to that of other Christians, I developed a performance mindset trying to earn my significance through good works.

> *Not that we [have the audacity to] venture to class or [even to] compare ourselves with some who exalt and furnish testimonials for themselves! However, when they measure themselves with themselves and compare themselves with one another, they are without understanding and behave unwisely* (2 Corinthians 10:12 AMP).

Freedom

When Jesus declared what His purpose for coming to earth was in Luke 4:18-19, it included proclaiming freedom to the prisoners:

*The Spirit of the Lord is on me, because He has anointed me to preach good news to the poor. He has sent me to **proclaim freedom** for the prisoners and recovery of sight for the blind, to release the oppressed, to proclaim the year of the Lord's favor.*

Then in John 8:36 Jesus said, *"If the Son sets **you free**, you will **be free** indeed."*

When I was in the pit of depression and despair, the cry of my heart was to live again. I felt I was locked in a prison of darkness and confusion and no one could help me escape. Even as we began to discover the root causes and deal with the issues that put me in that prison, there still seemed to be no clear pathway out. It seemed I was destined to go through life dragging a ball and chain filled with pills and confusion that would keep me from living a normal life.

I knew the Bible said Christ has given me freedom, but I needed to figure out how to apprehend it and then live in that freedom. As the Lord has so often done with me, I walked through the process personally and then He showed me the steps He had taken me through so I could share the process with others. Here is the process:

The ABCs of Running Free

Abiding: Abiding means remaining steadfast; to take up residence in. Jesus told His disciples in John 8:31-32 (AMP):

If you abide in My word [hold fast to My teachings and live in accordance with them], you are truly My disciples. And you will know the Truth, and the Truth will set you free.

Building: Building means to construct, to establish (strong, secure foundation needed).

For it is through Him [Christ] *that we both [whether far off or near] now have an introduction (access) by one [Holy] Spirit to the Father [so that we are able to approach Him]. Therefore you are no longer outsiders (exiles, migrants, and aliens, excluded from the rights of citizens), but you now share citizenship with the saints (God's own people, consecrated and set apart for Himself);* **and you belong to God's [own] household. You are built upon the foundation of the apostles and prophets with Christ Jesus Himself the chief Cornerstone** (Ephesians 2:18-20 AMP).

Conditioning: Conditioning means to bring into and keep in bodily health. The apostle Paul uses athletic competition to explain the need for conditioning if we want to run to win.

Do you not know that in a race all the runners compete, but [only] one receives the prize? So run [your race] that you may lay hold [of the prize] and make it yours. **Now every athlete who goes into training conducts himself temperately and restricts himself in all things.** *They do it to win a wreath that will soon wither, but we [do it to receive a crown of eternal blessedness] that cannot wither. Therefore I do not run uncertainly (without definite aim). I do not box like one beating the air and striking without an adversary* (1 Corinthians 9:24-26 AMP).

Discipline: Discipline means a field of learning, training to develop self-control or right conduct and follows closely on the shirttails of conditioning. First Corinthians 9:27 completes the athletic analogy described by Paul.

But [like a boxer] I buffet my body [handle it roughly, **discipline it** *by hardships] and subdue it, for fear that after proclaiming to* *others the Gospel and things pertaining to it, I myself should be-come unfit [not stand the test, be unapproved and rejected as a counterfeit]* (1 Corinthians 9:27 AMP).

Endurance: Endurance is the power to withstand stress and suffering, fortitude.

In Hebrews 12:1-2, Paul encourages us:

Run with patient endurance and steady and active persistence the appointed course of the race that is set before us, looking away [from all that will distract] to Jesus, Who is the Leader and the Source of our faith [giving the first incentive for our belief] and is also its Finisher [bringing it to maturity and perfection]. He, for the joy [of obtaining the prize] that was set before Him, endured the cross, despising and ignoring the shame, and is now seated at the right hand of the throne of God (Hebrews 12:1-2 AMP).

Finishing: Finishing means to arrive at the end of the race, task, or journey. I pray that all of us, like Paul can say, *"I have fought the good fight, I have finished the race, I have kept the faith"* (2 Tim. 4:7).

I have watched as Chrystal's whole life has changed since her healing from God. She has become more balanced in her life in general. She is still busy but balanced. She has a horse and takes time to balance out church life and leisure time. She takes time to get away, goes running, is involved in an exercise program, and regularly gets outside to enjoy the great outdoors. I see her as busy but not stressing out herself or others. She always seems to be balanced now, not perfect but definitely balanced.[8]

God Fulfills Another Dream

Though I never voiced my desire, God began to arrange for a desire deep in my heart to be met. I longed to ride again and secretly yearned for the possibility of someday owning my own horse. Ken and I were talking one day and he suggested I return to riding, since it had given me such pleasure, and that he would be open to buying a horse if the right one came along. While I was shocked and thrilled at the possibility of my dream coming true, I spent some time in prayer over the matter. I sensed the Lord saying to me that He never asked me to let go of my dream to own a horse; I had come to that conclusion on my own. He wanted me to ask Him to fulfill this desire of my heart.

I immediately called on my friend Linda to help with the search for a good horse. Now you are never supposed to buy a horse for its color because there are many things to take into consideration. Nevertheless I simply asked the Lord for a coal-black horse around the age of 12 to14 years. But I told the Lord I trusted Him and was willing to buy the horse that best suited my riding and confidence level. It took about a year of searching and trying out different horses before I found the one that I believed God had for me.

Linda called one day and said she found a horse that might meet my requirements. We went to the stables where the horse was boarded. Ace was a beautiful, coal-black seven-year-old. I rode him and began to really like him. When purchasing a horse, it is a good idea to have a veterinarian check the horse out for any unseen health problems. So I went through two vet checks that resulted in differing opinions concerning Ace's health. I was then left in a quandary of what to do and which one to believe. I didn't want to put our family in a financial strain because of my hobby, and yet I didn't want to pass up this horse if he truly was the one. I also wanted to be sure that this horse's mind was sound and that I would not get badly hurt through some accident caused by an unreliable horse.

So one afternoon I sat outside on my patio and just prayed asking God for wisdom on the matter, wanting to know if Ace was the horse He had chosen for me. In that quiet moment the Lord took me back seven years to the day Ken and I sat in the car at the forest preserve right at the beginning of the breakdown. We saw a lady riding a horse and Ken and I prayed that God would give me the opportunity to ride. He then reminded me that was the summer of 1996 and pointed out that Ace was foaled in the spring of 1996. I had thought He had answered our prayer by sending Linda and the opportunity to ride with her, but the Lord said He also answered the desire of my heart that day. It just took seven years to bring him to me. I just cried realizing God knew the desires of my heart and had prepared Ace for me from my first whispered prayer.

> When our season of riding together was over and Chrystal and Ken decided to try and find her a horse of her own, I connected her with a friend of mine who had a horse that I thought fit her requirements. At first he was asking more than their budget would allow, so we looked elsewhere. But he discovered he couldn't sell it for what he was asking and decided he wanted Ace to have a good home. He had raised the horse himself. God provided the perfect horse for Crystal—even the color she had mentioned she had wanted.[9]

Now every time I ride Ace I am reminded of the love of a Father who knows how to give good gifts to His children. Ace is my God-gift and I remind him all the time that he was created and given to me by our Creator. I realize that God is using my relationship with Ace to help me learn more about Him as well. The relationship between a horse and its owner has many parallels to the relationship we have with our heavenly Father. Just like the Father wants us to cooperate with His ways and plans, I want Ace to cooperate with me. When he doesn't, I have to get stern and sometimes inflict a measure of discomfort to get my message across. My heart is for us to enjoy our time together. I want Ace to trust me and know that I will take care of him and that where I lead him will be safe.

That's what the Father's heart is toward us. He wants us to trust Him with our lives and willingly go where He leads us, resting in His care and guidance. The truth is that only when we allow Him to lead us can we be totally transformed and made whole.

My Adventure and Journey With God

1. Look up and write out the following Scriptures:

   Matthew 19:26

   Mark 10:27

   Luke 18:27

2. What appears to be impossible for you but possible for God?

3. Read Mark 11:12-20. Be encouraged to continue to believe for the possible with God.

4. Read Romans 12:2, it speaks of God transforming us into a new person by changing the way we think. Ask the Lord to show you the changes He desires to bring to your thinking. List them below:

_____

_____

_____

_____

5. We can be raised as a Christian and grow up in church and still not truly understand how significant we are to the Father. Take a moment and reflect on your level of security in Christ and the depth of your significance as being Christ's child. Journal your thoughts and need for more of Him in these areas.

6. What are the ABCs of running free?

    A_____ Reference: _____

    B_____ Reference: _____

    C_____ Reference: _____

    D_____ Reference: _____

    E_____ Reference: _____

    F_____ Reference: _____

    Which of these do you need to ask Christ to work more deeply into your life?

7. Personalize Psalm 139:13-17 by writing your name in the blanks. Then read it out loud to yourself as your prayer for this chapter.

*For You formed [_____] inward
parts; You wove [_____]
in my mother's womb. I will give thanks to You, for I
[_____] am fearfully and
wonderfully made; wonderful are Your works, and my soul knows
it very well. [_____] frame
was not hidden from You, when I was made in secret, and skill-
fully wrought in the depths of the earth; Your eyes have seen
[_____] unformed substance;
and in Your book were all written. The days that were ordained
for [_____], when as yet there
was not one of them. How precious also are Your thoughts to
[_____], O God! How vast is the sum
of them!* (Psalm 139:13-17 NASB)

8. What dream of yours has God fulfilled? Or write
   below what dream you are asking Him to fulfill? Give
   thanks for the answer and for the answer on the way.

   _____

   _____

   _____

   _____

CHAPTER 9

ALIGNED FOR LIVING

I HAVE A HEART FOR PEOPLE who struggle emotionally and are impaired mentally, who are discouraged and tormented because their rational minds don't work right. I have worked with a lot of people who have struggled for years because their doctors want to medicate their symptoms and the church wants to pray it away, denying the role of the medical field in their healing.

I know that part of the healing God gave me was a physical healing because there was a physical chemical imbalance in my brain. If we have a problem with our heart or our liver and it doesn't function well, we need to deal with it in the physical realm. When we have a problem in our brain and it's not functioning normally, we need a physical solution as well. God also dealt with the hurt and pain of my life and touched me there spiritually.

I believe God wants to minister to the whole person. He wants to bring transformation to every part of our body, our soul, and our spirit. I believe that's why my experience was so unique, because each of these three areas received ministry. I believe that by sharing my experience, others will realize what can be done to receive a total transformation in Christ Jesus. Scripture tells us that He heals the broken spirit, He restores to life our mortal bodies, and makes new the attitude of our minds (see Isa. 61:1 AMP; Rom. 8:11 AMP; Eph. 4:23).

Total Transformation

Total transformation is God transforming the whole person: body, soul, and spirit. It's not just a spiritual element. It's not just about us becoming stronger believers—though that's a very important aspect. When we look through Scripture, we find that the Lord talks about our physical strength as well as our spiritual strength. The Bible also says we will prosper as our soul prospers (see 3 John 2 NASB).

The Bible talks about the renewing of the mind and our ability to make right choices (see Rom. 12:2). We can learn to have our will cooperate with God's plan and our emotions come into right relationship with the Lord (see Hebrews 13:20-21). I believe transformation is really about the ministry that Christ set out to do from the very beginning of His earthly ministry. In Luke 4:18-19, when Jesus read the passage out of Isaiah, He was defining His earthly ministry.

The Spirit of the Lord God is upon me, because the Lord has anointed and qualified me to **preach the Gospel of good tidings** *to the meek, the poor, and afflicted; He has sent me to bind up and* **heal the brokenhearted,** *to* **proclaim liberty** *to the [physical and spiritual]* *captives and the* **opening** *of the prison and* *of the eyes to those who are bound, to proclaim the acceptable year of the Lord [the year of His favor] and the day of vengeance of our God, to comfort all who mourn* (Isaiah 61:1-2 AMP).

When Jesus says that the Spirit of the Lord is upon Him to preach good news, He is talking about the salvation news for our spirit. Jesus also said He was sent to heal those who were afflicted or sick and to open blind eyes. That's the body or physical realm of healing. When He says He was sent to heal the brokenhearted and comfort all who mourn, He is referring to the need for emotional healing for the soul.

The ministry of Jesus was to transform the whole man: body, soul, and spirit. The word *transformation* denotes a complete change of form, appearance, nature, or function. I personally experienced that three-fold healing from the Lord. He healed my body, He's renewing my mind, and in the spiritual realm I'm becoming more Christlike because of what He's doing deep inside my heart. Proverbs tells us that we do need a healing if our heart has been broken because *"heartache crushes the spirit"* (Prov. 15:13; see also Prov. 18:14).

The problem is that we forget that it's more than just knowing the Scriptures and head knowledge that brings about a total healing. We can memorize all the Scriptures and quote whole chapters of the Bible; but if we have not experienced that truth for ourselves in our own lives, we will not live in the possession of God's promises. The Word of God tells us that faith without works is dead (see James 2:17-18). That means we may have to act on what we believe even before it is manifested in the physical. I had to learn that lesson personally before I could move toward a total healing and wholeness.

For with the heart a person believes (adheres to, trusts in, and re-lies on Christ) and so is justified (declared righteous, acceptable to God), and with the mouth he confesses (declares openly and speaks out freely his faith) and confirms [his] salvation. The Scripture says, No man who believes in Him [who adheres to, relies on, and trusts in Him] will [ever] be put to shame or be disappointed (Romans 10:10-11 AMP).

Heal the Brokenhearted

I've discovered that there are two types of trauma that can cause a broken heart. One is when we are denied the good things we all need growing up, such as not being cherished by our parents. The second type is when bad things happen, such as physical or mental abuse.

Scripture reveals the depth of suffering we can experience from a broken heart.

Heartache *crushes the spirit* (Proverbs 15:13).

A crushed spirit who can bear? (Proverbs 18:14)

Search me, O God, and know my heart; test me and know my **anxious thoughts** (Psalm 139:23).

Anxiety *in a man's heart weighs it down* (Proverbs 12:25 AMP).

It becomes very difficult to serve the Lord and use the talents and gifts He has placed in us when we are suffering from a broken heart.

A happy heart is good medicine and a cheerful mind works healing, but a broken spirit dries up the bones (Proverbs 17:22 AMP).

All the days of the desponding and afflicted are made evil [by **anxious thoughts and forebodings**], *but he who has a glad heart has a continual feast* **[regardless of circumstances]** (Proverbs 15:15 AMP).

Given the choice between the two, most of us would choose a happy heart. Jesus said He came to heal the brokenhearted, so we know there is a way to access that healing.

The secret to moving toward healing, no matter where or how that trauma and pain occurred, is in the way we respond to God's process. First of all, are we willing to allow God to search our hearts and unveil the hidden wound?

The death of my paternal grandfather virtually lanced open the wound I had in my heart concerning the death of my father. At the time, I thought God was incredibly cruel to add that pain to what I was already experiencing. Part of my move toward total healing was to learn how to respond to the pain and grief that was revealed during this "God surgery" on my heart.

Responding to Pain and Grief

God provided Christian doctors to care for me during this difficult time in my life. They gave me the hope that God could do a miracle despite their diagnosis, and that His grace would enable and sustain me to walk through whatever was ahead of me. With that support in place, God provided a spiritual father and mother to walk alongside my family and me and minister to all of us as the Lord led them. It wasn't until after I had received my healing that I learned they had come to our congregation through a direct word from the Lord about a woman who was going to need their love and care. What an awesome God who leads and directs the steps of His children precisely to minister for Him!

The love and care of this precious couple began to minister to an area of my heart and life that carried great pain, deep grief, and sadness. I had never before opened this place to anyone. This inner place was where I held feelings and emotions that were so powerful, I was afraid to look at them. But when the Lord sent people to me who knew and understood God's transforming power, I began to open up gradually and let God work healing in my heart through their gentle and persistent guidance.

I learned that it was all right to respond with confusion and anger as long as I was willing to talk it through with God and those He placed in my life to help me. I learned that those were times I would begin to move forward and grow. I learned from experience that suppressing these questions and emotions only leads to a downward spiral. Seeking the right kind of help brings healing and leads to a productive instead of a destructive lifestyle.

David's writings in the Psalms help us to honestly face our true feelings and speak about them honestly, while at the same time acknowledging our need for God's help to overcome the potentially negative effect on our lives.

Look at Psalm 6:1-2. David is basically asking the Lord not to get angry with him if he openly shares his heart. David also acknowledges that God is the one who has to do the healing of his inner pain.

O Lord, rebuke me not in Your anger nor discipline and chasten me in Your hot displeasure. Have mercy on me and be gracious to me, O Lord, for I am weak (faint and withered away); O Lord, heal me, for my bones are troubled (Psalm 6:1-2 AMP).

In verses 3-7, David honestly tells God exactly how he is feeling and that he thinks God has abandoned him to his pain and grief.

> *My [inner] self [as well as my body] is also exceedingly disturbed and troubled. But You, O Lord, how long [until You return and speak peace to me]? Return [to my relief], O Lord, deliver my life; save me for the sake of Your steadfast love and mercy. ...I am weary with my groaning; all night I soak my pillow with tears, I drench my couch with my weeping. My eye grows dim because of grief* (Psalm 6:3-7 AMP).

Verses 8 and 9 tell us that God responded to David's cries: *"The Lord has heard the voice of my weeping. The Lord has heard my supplication; the Lord receives my prayer"* (AMP).

David's writings reveal to us that he did not try to hide his emotions from God. They express the full range of emotions David was experiencing, including distress, sadness, despair, anger, and envy. But they also reveal his heart's desire to praise and worship the Lord. That's why I love David. He was able to look into the deep parts of his soul and say, "God, I feel like death has entangled me in this situation, and I've cried out to You."

My spiritual mentors helped me to see that I could open up the recesses of my heart and I could look at the deep places where I was confused, disappointed, upset, and disillusioned. As I did, God met me there because He is close to the brokenhearted. He comforts those whose spirits are crushed. His way always leads to giving life to His beloved children.

> The pain and the grief of losing her father were very real and intense. I observed the Lord speak to Chrystal and help her deal with saying good-bye to her father with the hope of

seeing him once again in Heaven. I watched as her healing progressed and saw how she could enjoy the sense of being who she was and not have the grief and sadness she once felt. I watched as the Lord helped her to see things as they are through the eyes of a mature adult and not as a child seeking approval and looking for someone else to give her a sense of being grounded.[1]

"I Told God I Was Angry"

I told God I was angry;
I thought He'd be surprised.
I thought I'd kept hostility
Quite cleverly disguised.

I told the Lord I hate Him;
I told Him that I hurt.
I told Him that He isn't fair;
He's treated me like dirt.

I told God I was angry,
but I'm the one surprised.
"What I've known all along," He said,
"You've finally realized.

"At last you have admitted
What's really in your heart:
Dishonesty, not anger,
Was keeping us apart.

"For even when you hate Me,
I don't stop loving you.
Before you can receive that love,
You must confess what's true.

"In telling me the anger
You genuinely feel,
It loses power over you
Permitting you to heal."

I told God I was sorry,
And He's forgiven me.
The truth that I was angry
Has finally set me free.

—Author Unknown

God's Way

Some Christians find this a tough concept to embrace. If we are really going to help anyone else, we must first look at our own hurt and pain. We've worked hard all of our lives to perfect our masks to keep others from getting too close to the truth about us. I worked so hard to hide all of my inner turmoil that it drove me into a psychotic breakdown. God wants to teach us a way to not only heal our broken hearts but live life to the fullest. *"There is a way that seems right to a man, but in the end it leads to death"* (Prov. 14:12). *"In his heart a man plans his course, but the Lord determines his steps"* (Prov. 16:9).

God wants us to get rid of our masks and be honest with ourselves. Through searching our hearts and exposing the areas of pain and trauma, we can invite the truth and wisdom of God to bring about change from the inside out. Psalm 51:6 again shows David had revelation that will help us in this quest for healing. Let us say with David, *"Behold, You desire truth in the inner being; make me therefore to know wisdom in my inmost heart"* (Ps. 51:6 AMP). When we willingly submit and allow God to search our hearts and to reveal what He finds to us, we open ourselves up to a healing above and beyond what we could even think or imagine.

In the last 14 years, this process has been unfolding in my life. The Holy Spirit has taken me places I would not have gone if left to my own devices. God has revealed areas I would have preferred to remain under lock and key. During this time, I often doubted myself, my calling, and my relationship with God. Nevertheless, I chose to remain faithful to Him regardless of my feeling. I made a conscious choice to proclaim as David did, *"I said to the Lord, 'You are my Lord; apart from You I have no good thing'"* (Ps. 16:2).

Even when I was at my lowest point, God assured me He was there and had not forsaken me. My mentors encouraged me that there was a plan in place for me, even though I could not see or understand it at the time.

> *"For I know the plans I have for you,"* declares the Lord, *"plans to prosper you and not to harm you, plans to give you hope and a future"* (Jeremiah 29:11).

> *As for God, His way is perfect; the word of the Lord is flawless. He is a shield for all who take refuge in Him* (Psalm 18:30).

Someone once wrote:

> *God hath not promised skies ever blue,*
> *Flower-strewn pathways always for you.*

God hath not promised sun without rain,
Joy without sorrow, peace without pain.
But He hath promised strength from above,
Unfailing sympathy, undying love.

Harboring Unbelief

Scripture also reveals that there can be places in our hearts that harbor unbelief. As I strove to overcome my confusion and pain, I found myself comparing my circumstances with those of other Christians and wondering why I wasn't living in the joy of the Lord like they were. I began to feel that God was unfair. As I allowed these thoughts to prevail, I moved closer and closer to a crisis of faith.

The Psalm writer Asaph in Psalm 73 reveals that he dealt with similar feelings, but the difference was that he openly shared them with God while I tried to hide them in the recesses of my heart:

> But as for me, my feet came close to stumbling, my steps had almost slipped. For I was envious of the arrogant as I saw the prosperity of the wicked (Psalm 73:2-3 NASB).

Then he shares his attitude about this and his temptation to lose faith:

> Behold, these are the ungodly, who always prosper and are at ease in the world; they increase in riches. Surely then in vain have I cleansed my heart and washed my hands in innocency. For all the day long have I been smitten and plagued, and chastened every morning (Psalm 73:12-14 AMP).

In Hebrews 3:12-13, the apostle Paul warns us about harboring such unbelief in our hearts. He says it will eventually cause us to harden our hearts toward God. Had I not had the support and encouragement of my husband and our church, I may well have kept everything hidden deep inside my heart and eventually turned away from God.

> See to it, brothers, that none of you has a sinful, unbelieving heart that turns away from the living God. But encourage one another daily, as long as it is called Today, so that none of you may be hardened by sin's deceitfulness (Hebrews 3:12-13).

Soul Man

Emotions can open the door to some hard questions when we are dealing with pain and grief. Is there any real purpose to my pain? If God loves me, then why doesn't He do something about this? If God is just, then why do the unjust seem to win and prosper?

The answer to these questions is not what most people think. As unpleasant as pain is while we are in the midst of it, pain has a purpose. Physical pain reveals the fact that a problem exists somewhere in our physical body. Emotional pain alerts us to the fact that something is wrong and needs to be dealt with in our souls. If we neglect to respond to the physical pain and find the cause, we can end up with a potentially life-threatening condition. Treating a fever with aspirin is merely dealing with the symptom and often keeps us from finding the true cause of an infection. The same is true in the emotional realm.

"I don't want to go there" are words often spoken out of fear of pain or shame. We may seek to flee from the feelings inside of us, when in truth we need to look deep inside our souls and speak honestly and frankly before God. Left to fester deep within us, these painful emotions can cause a "cancer" to grow that will eventually permeate every aspect of our lives. The problem is, most of us have been taught to suppress our negative feelings.

As a lifelong Christian and a pastor's wife, I felt I was not supposed to be experiencing depression or the other range of emotions I seemed to be having. I slipped into a performance mentality to "earn" my healing and be a "better" Christian. Each of us has our own way to try to dull the intensity of emotions raging inside of us. If we are not allowed to release them, a volcano will erupt, possibly damaging not only our own lives but the lives of those closest to us.

We have a great High Priest who has personally experienced everything we will ever have to face. Hebrews 4:15 reminds us:

> *For we do not have a High Priest Who is unable to understand and sympathize and have a shared feeling with our weaknesses and infirmities and liability to the assaults of temptation, but One Who has been tempted in every respect as we are, yet without sinning* (Hebrews 4:15 AMP).

Jesus experienced a full range of emotions as He prayed to the Father in the Garden of Gethsemane. *"My Father, if it is possible, may this cup be taken from Me. Yet not as I will, but as You will"* (Matt. 26:39). Jesus surrendered His will to the Father. He desired a different outcome to the circumstances in His life, but He knew that the Father's way was best. In the same way, we must be willing to walk through our circumstances the way the Father chooses for us, learning how to abandon our own selfish desires.

Jesus surrendered His mind and emotions to the Father by aligning Himself with the ways of His Father. As we learn how to align our whole self to the Father's way, our thoughts, emotions, and will come under the Father's influence.

Lean on, trust in, and be confident in the Lord with all your heart and mind and do not rely on your own insight or understanding. In all your ways know, recognize, and acknowledge Him, and He will direct and make straight and plain your paths (Proverbs 3:5-6 AMP).

When the medicine stopped working and I surrendered myself to God, I opened the door for Him to come in and take my healing on the path He had chosen. When I declared I was willing to continue to serve Him whether He completely healed me or not, I surrendered my will to His way. I am a living testimony of the transforming power of Christ. His first work of transformation in my life began at salvation. Then He patiently brought me to a place where I would allow Him to heal my broken heart. He broke the chains that had imprisoned me and released me from the bondages of heaviness and depression. Then His touch healed my physical body and He brought me to a place of peace I had never before experienced. I thought I just wanted to be normal. He gave me so much more than what I thought I wanted!

Quest for Peace

It seems that mankind will do anything to find peace and a sense of inner rest for their souls. Peace is, in our culture, the most sought-after commodity of mental health, yet remains the most elusive. Sadly, even the Church has failed in fully engaging in this commodity. As a result, New Age spiritualism and materialism have become common ways that man has tried to bring a sense of inner peace to a hectic, fast-paced world. The problem is, these substitutes are temporary and eventually result in the need to search for another way to calm our restless souls.

Philippians 4:7 tells us, *"The peace of God, which transcends all under-standing, will guard your hearts and your minds in Christ Jesus."* In dealing with depression, peace is one of the things that seems farthest from us. It is the very thing we run after, yet it eludes us if we seek it in the wrong direction. In John 14:27, Jesus told His disciples:

> *Peace I leave with you; My [own] peace I now give and bequeath to you. Not as the world gives do I give to you. Do not let your hearts be troubled, neither let them be afraid. [Stop allowing yourselves to be agitated and disturbed; and do not permit yourselves to be fearful and intimidated and cowardly and unsettled]* (John 14:27 AMP).

In order to experience peace, there must be healing deep in our souls. To the extent we are healed is the extent we experience peace. The peace of God is ever present; however, our ability to experience it is based on the wholeness within our souls. When we refuse to allow healing to come to our wounded hearts, many misconceptions appear, which result in pain, suffering, and depression.

Many of us define peace as keeping everything under control as we become successful stress managers. The problem with this approach is that in order to keep stress from affecting us, we have to harden our hearts or retreat from reality. I found I could only go so long trying to be a stress manager, and then I would have to retreat from everyone and everything until I felt in control again. Those times began to come more frequently, until I got to a point that I was afraid I would never find my way back to reality.

I believe peace is a state of relaxed contentment and confidence, knowing and resting in the Father's love. Within this confidence and rest any circumstance or situation is manageable and able to be conquered for Kingdom purposes. When we have emotional baggage, we cannot attain the full peace that God intends for us; thus, we become caught in the throes of depression and despair. Then we add guilt to all the other negative emotions we are feeling because a Christian is supposed to be able to rest in God's peace. What results is a treadmill-type existence. We exhaust ourselves trying to earn that peace but never seem to get any closer to it.

Avoiding the Circumstance Trap

Without God's peace, we are vulnerable to circumstance possession. This is the result of looking at the circumstances around us as threatening. We will respond to this with fear, worry, sadness, or anger. When we look at our circumstances only from a natural point of view, it disturbs our thoughts and robs us of God's promised peace. We allow the "what ifs" to rob us of today's peace. We get so busy battling our circumstances that we never achieve a sense of peace. At the end of the day, this can become so overwhelming that the brain either can't rest enough to let us sleep or it begins to move toward a total shutdown, making it difficult to wake from sleep.

The healthier alternative to the first view is to look at circumstances through God's perspective. The key is to realize that God is in control and is continually working all things for our good as we cooperate with His plans according to His ways (see Rom. 8:28). Peace can only be found within this viewpoint.

We hinder ourselves in this quest for peace by refusing to align ourselves with what God desires to do in us. We know that within our souls lies much that God desires to touch and heal. We choose to cooperate and receive all that is promised by the Father through the Son to us, His children. We can access that peace that surpasses all understanding, which will guard our hearts and minds in Christ Jesus (see Phil. 4:7). When we find ourselves in the pit of depression, we long for a peace in both our hearts and minds.

> You can't be connected with God until you're at peace with who you are. If you're still upset that God gave you this body or this life or this family or these circumstances, you will never be able to connect with God in a healthy, thriving, sustainable sort of way. You'll be at odds with your Maker. And if you can't come to terms with who you are and the life you've been given, you'll never be able to accept others and how they were made and the lives they've been given. And until you're at peace with God and those around you, you will continue to struggle with your role on the planet, your part to play in the ongoing creation of the universe.[2]

The Pit of Depression

I waited patiently and expectantly for the Lord; and He inclined to me and heard my cry. He drew me up out of a horrible pit [a pit of tumult and of destruction], out of the miry clay (froth and slime), and set my feet upon a rock, steadying my steps and establishing my goings. And He has put a new song in my mouth, a song of praise to our God. Many shall see and fear (revere and worship) and put their trust and confident reliance in the Lord (Psalm 40:1-3 AMP).

Depression at any level brings debilitating effects to everyday life and activities. To effectively climb out of this pit of depression we need to understand how it affects our entire being. We have already learned that man is a three-part being; therefore, to become aligned for living we must achieve healing in all three parts: body, soul, and spirit.

The Physical Effects of Depression Are Very Real

The experience of depression varies widely from person to person, yet there are common threads and statements that descriptively explain the physical effects of depression on the body:

- "My head feels like it will explode."

- "My heart hurts; it feels like it will stop beating."

- "My head feels stuffy, and I have no energy."

- "My entire body is wracked with pain. It feels like a thousand knives are being driven into me at the same time."

- "I have a dull ache in my chest and abdomen."

- "My body feels heavy, slow, and hard to move in doing ordinary tasks."

Other physical symptoms the body can experience could include weight loss or weight gain, nausea, constipation, diarrhea, and muscle spasms. I remember hitting my head against the wall trying to alleviate the intense pain in my head. There were many instances during my illness that left me feeling as if I couldn't move because my body felt so weighed down and heavy. There were times when nothing I did could ease the physical pain I was feeling.

The Soul: the Mind, the Emotions, and the Will Are Very Much Affected by Depression

Feelings such as hopelessness, uselessness, sadness, and loneliness can turn to irritability and anger for no apparent reason. The thought process slows down, making it hard to think, and making the depressed person feel disorganized, anxious, and tense. The following statements clearly show the state of mind that a depressed person is in:

- "I put on a mask and act like nothing is wrong."

- "I sometimes sit and stare at the wall for hours while crying."

- "I feel like someone placed a clamp on my brain and has thrown a thick blanket over it, making everything grind to a halt."

- "I feel like I'm in a fog and cannot see my way out. It's frightening."

- "I feel like a non-person; life feels meaningless."

- "I have lost all feeling for my family."

- "I am alive physically but not mentally."

Don't Try to Convince Them Otherwise—They Can't Fathom It Being Any Different

I know, I've been there and know firsthand how frightening being in the pit of depression can be. There were times I could not tell if it was day or night. I wasn't sure if what I was seeing was real or imagined. Many times I walked around in a fog for days and could not remember anything that happened during that entire time frame.

Truly the Spirit of One in Depression Is Crushed, Causing an Acute Loss of Hope

Probably the most devastating effect of depression on the spirit is losing the desire to converse with God. There is an inward cry to God to rescue them and an intense anger at God when they do not see the expected response from Him. These statements reflected my attitude toward God while I was at the bottom of the pit of depression:

- "I don't sense God or feel Him."

- "What if God doesn't touch or heal me?"

- "God's promises aren't true for me."

- "Is God really real, or just a figment of my imagination?"

- "How could God love me in this state? I can't be the Christian I should be."

- "If I was a strong Christian I would find a way out of this."

- "Why won't God deliver me or fix me?"

- "If God really loved me, He would do something."

Obviously, all three parts of humans are deeply affected by depression. In order to start the climb out of that horrible pit, the depressed person must begin taking responsibility for certain aspects in each of these three parts.

The Responsibilities of the Depressed

Taking responsibility is no easy task and often seems impossible when you are looking up from the bottom of the pit of depression. Nevertheless, responsibility is the component needed to begin the process of climbing out of the pit of despair. If *responsibility* is not taken, one will remain caught and snared by the tentacles of depression.

Depressed individuals often neglect to carry out the most basic routines of everyday living. Improving your basic health is essential to dealing with depression. Here are some basic ideas to begin:

- Take a multivitamin.

- Eat nourishing foods.

- Drink a healthy supplement drink.

- Exercise. (It raises the level of endorphins, which are natural pain relievers, and lifts your spirits emotionally.)

- Get enough rest.

Making any kind of change from a normal routine takes practice, even when you are not depressed. For the person who is depressed, these simple changes may seem overwhelming. A loved one may need to take charge and be responsible for implementing change for the one in depression. I relied heavily on my husband and caring friends to make sure I took vitamins and got enough rest, especially during my hyperactive episodes. When I could not remember whether I had eaten or not, others took over and monitored my eating habits. When I was afraid to leave the house for fear I would have an episode of some kind, loved ones offered to be my companion and helped keep me from becoming a recluse.

The family who offered to let me ride their horses as often as I wanted became a particular blessing in ministering to my physical needs as well as my emotional ones. Nurturing a healthy, stable mind is very important to progressing toward wholeness and freedom. The power of thought is life-altering. We must take responsibility to focus our thoughts on the truth of what God is saying and has said about us. Here are some simple things to do in the arena of filling the mind with God's truth:

- Regularly talk with good counselors (whether professional or spiritual).

- Positive company; choose wisely who you surround yourself with. (If there are negative and discouraging individuals in your life—distance yourself from them.)

- Feed your mind with encouraging music, movies, TV shows, and books.

- Recite Scripture verses of hope and promise.

- Use positive self-talk on a regular basis.

The influence of words and positive company plays a crucial role in one's outlook and mind-set. To the depressed person, words and positive interaction are a crucial component in healing and recovery. Being surrounded by uplifting and encouraging people goes a long way in this healing process. I was so blessed by the support and encouraging words I received from our congregation when I had to withdraw from all church activity.

Along with this must come positive and truthful self-talk. This can be difficult enough for one without depression, but with it, this can be a very excruciating experience. Negative and untruthful self-talk leads to bondages, whereas the truth of God's Word brings freedom. After receiving the healing from the Lord, I would get up in the morning, look at myself in the mirror, and say, "I thank You, Lord, for my healing; just bring my body into alignment." I was not denying the fact that my body was in pain but I acknowledged that God had the answer and was greater than what was happening to me physically.

What feeds your spirit is as important as what feeds your body. Depressed people often stop all of the activities that they once enjoyed and found fulfilling. Even though I had to force myself to leave the house, my weekly horseback riding fed my spirit in a way nothing else could. God also sent me His handpicked mentors to give me prayer support and covering as well as help me understand what God was doing in my life. Nurturing your spirit is so important because it is your spirit man that gives you life and meaning. If your spirit is nurtured you can gain the strength and motivation to work on the other areas as well.

I believe it is the role of the Body of Christ to provide a safe place for those trapped in the pit of depression. We need to help these struggling Christians find the kind of assistance they need to climb up out of that horrible dark pit. My prayer is that through sharing what I learned through my own climb up out of that pit, we can all begin to work together to bring healing to the multitudes of depressed people sitting in our congregations. The remaining few chapters of this book will discuss depression in the Church and how to more effectively minister to those trapped in the pit of depression and mental illness.

My Adventure and Journey With God

1. The ministry of Jesus was to transform the whole man: body, soul, and spirit. The word *transformation* denotes a complete change of form, appearance, nature, or function. List ways your life has been transformed by God's power. Then list the areas that still need His power to touch and transform.

2. Let us say with David, *"Behold, You desire truth in the inner being; make me therefore to know wisdom in my inmost heart"* (Ps. 51:6 AMP). When we willingly submit and allow God to search our hearts and to reveal what He finds to us, we open ourselves up to a healing above and beyond what

we could even think or imagine. Return once again to the poem "Only You" in the introduction. Pray it once again, asking for God to penetrate your heart deeply. What new depths of your heart have been revealed to you since you began reading this book?

3. Read John 14:27 and reflect on how deep the peace of God penetrates your heart and life. What areas do you desire for His peace to penetrate? List them and bring them before the Lord in prayer.

4. In reading this saying, what do you receive personally for your life and the circumstances you are dealing with?

> *God hath not promised skies ever blue,*
> *Flower-strewn pathways always for you.*
> *God hath not promised sun without rain,*
> *Joy without sorrow, peace without pain.*
> *But He hath promised strength from above,*
> *Unfailing sympathy, undying love.*

5. Use the following Scriptures to begin a routine of renewing your mind:

Psalm 34:4 says I am: _____

Philippians 4:13 says I am: _____

John 15:9 says I am: _____

Hebrews 13:5-6 says I am: _____

Romans 8:16-17 says I am: _____

6. Pray and ask the Lord to give you the strength to begin taking responsibility for implementing good health routines, surrounding yourself with positive people, and daily reading Scriptures on hope.

CHAPTER 10

DEPRESSION IN THE CHURCH

I HAVE BEEN AMAZED at the epidemic of depression that seems to exist among congregations and leaders. In sharing my testimony, I am constantly amazed by the number of people who shared with me how they have suffered in silence with some level of depression or mental illness. They all expressed a similar feeling of isolation and echoed a statement I have heard all too often in the Body of Christ: "I've stopped taking my medication because I feel if I take it I have no faith." May God help us to deal more effectively with those who are caught in the throes of depression and its very real effect on their lives.

For those who are going through depression or are dealing with others in the midst of it, I highly recommend an article given to me at Emerge Ministries titled, "Heart Cry: A Biblical Model of Depression" by David P. Armentrout.[1]

In 1990 almost 11 million adult Americans suffered a clinical depression. Even more disturbing than depression having already reached epidemic levels, is the fact that it is still increasing. Once a person experiences an episode of major depression he or she has an increased probability of experiencing a second episode. Research has also found that there was a pattern of increasing severity from the original episode to the succeeding first, second and third relapse episodes. If we are to stem the apparent rising tide, we must act with understanding, using interventions based on the total of what we know, rather than relying on any single source. First, depression is seen as a state of mind, body and spirit.[2]

One of the biggest problems is that the churches don't know what to do about mental illness and depression. Therefore, they are doing a grave disservice to believers who suffer from these very real illnesses. As a believer, minister and a pastor's wife, it was very hard for me to go to the church body and share what was going on in my life. I was very blessed to be part of a church family who embraced me and was there to encourage and protect me, but many in the Body of Christ do not have this support available to them. As disciples of Jesus, I believe we are to minister to the whole person and that the Church should be a safe haven for all who suffer physically, mentally, emotionally, or spiritually.

Depressed people need a safe place to heal from hurt and pain. Every person I've talked to who has suffered with depression, or any kind of mental illness, has a story of pain, loss, or wounding, and they have struggled for answers. The general responses from the Church have been: pray a little harder, be strong in the Lord, and remember you're victorious in Christ. What we need to do is encourage the wounded to pour out their hearts to the Lord and let Him heal in whatever way He chooses. God sent me a Christian psychiatrist, a Christian psychologist, and a spiritual mentor. Then He finished the healing Himself at His appointed time and place.

The biggest revelation I gained out of my experience of mental illness is the knowledge of how God loved me even when I couldn't love Him back. I know without a shadow of a doubt that when I'm physically, emotionally, and spiritually unable to love Him, He still loves me. It's so simple, yet we try to make it so complex. We believe we've got to perform to get God's approval and earn His love, but that is as far from the truth as the east is from the west. The Bible says that *"while we were yet sinners,"* even when we were enemies of God, *"Christ died for us,"* demonstrating His great love for us (Rom. 5:8 NASB; see also Rom. 5:6-11).

Mental illness affects everyone in the family, not just the "sick" person. We, as the Body of Christ, must also be equipped to minister to the whole family as well as the whole person. Once I had been set free, Ken and I turned our attention to our children, keeping an eye open for any of the negative debris from the illness they were exposed to. We discovered Reneé had picked up a spirit of fear as she worried about whether Mommy would ever get well. We sat down with her and explained how God had healed me and that she did not have to worry anymore. We prayed with her and saw a marked improvement, especially in her sleep habits.

We discovered we needed to go even deeper into this spirit of fear issue in our then 11-year-old daughter. God took us back to the events surrounding Reneé's birth to help us understand how to help bring total healing to our daughter in this area.

Just before Reneé was born, I began to hyperventilate, causing my body and my baby to be deprived of oxygen. Reneé's heart rate dropped, and she was born blue. Everyone in the room was afraid we might lose her. When she took that first breath and we saw that she could breathe on her own, we all thanked God for preserving her little life. What we did not understand at the time was that fear permeated that whole delivery room and found its way into little Reneé's spirit. Once we realized this was the real root of the fear she was dealing with, we explained her birth to her and how God had watched over her even then and that He was still watching over her and our whole family. We prayed a very simple prayer with her. She no longer deals with the spirit of fear.

The Church needs to be equipped to provide the environment and resources so wounded and broken Christians and their families can receive the right kind of help and guidance to achieve healing. I want us to have some biblical insights that will move us in that direction. Jesus told us that if we know God's truth, that truth will set us free (see John 8:32).

> A heart response to grief or sadness can be caused by a variety of events and experiences, both within and/or external to ourselves—psychological, social, and spiritual events. In response to heart-sorrow, there is a corresponding action that leads to either healing and strengthening or intensified feelings of hopelessness and powerlessness. Together thoughts and feelings interact with behavior. *The treatment plan should then reflect spiritual, physiological, social and psychological interventions as well as dealing with the possible medical causes.*[3]

Being Honest With Ourselves

As I look back on the progression of both my illness and my healing, the turning point for me was when I honestly told God what I was feeling in my heart. However, it took me a long time to come to that point because it was not an acceptable behavior for a believer. God led me to read the songs and poems of the person He described as *"a man after My own heart"* (Acts 13:22; see also 1 Sam. 13:14). Not only did God allow David to openly share his heart, He didn't get angry over the frustration and confusion David confessed he was feeling.

David was a master at pouring his heart out to the Lord in a very honest and straightforward way. "God, here's where I'm at. I don't know where You are right now, but my enemies are all around me wanting to destroy me. The cords of death entangle me and I'm in anguish every night crying out to You" (see Ps. 18:4). David was able to tell God exactly how he really felt.

David was also able to pull from the reserve already deposited in his spirit man and say, "I will bless You, Lord; You are my refuge, and You are my strength" (see Ps. 18:1-3). We need to do both. We need to be very honest with God about what we are feeling. "I don't get You; I don't understand what You are doing here. It seems like what You're doing is cruel and that makes me angry at You." But at the same time we need to admit: "Where else am I going to go? I have no other good thing. God, You are the only thing I have. You have got to be my refuge and my strength." We must learn to both acknowledge our spirit man, who God is and be willing to admit what's going on in our hearts, our soul man.

As we move toward healing, we must be able to admit to ourselves and to God, "I am weak, I am struggling, I need help." The mind-set of most Christians is to battle in secret and not admit we need help. We believe only when we have battled through to the end are we to share our testimony of how we attained victory. The problem with this kind of thinking is that anything we try to hold in secret, especially something we consider a weakness or crack in our armor, gives the enemy a foothold in our lives. The Bible warns us about allowing the enemy any kind of foothold in our lives (see Eph. 4:27).

Anyone who knows something about you that you do not want anyone else to find out holds a measure of power over you. He or she can virtually blackmail you into doing things you really don't want to do. That person can then become a very powerful influence in your life. The enemy loves to threaten us with anything we think other Christians might hold against us or that would bring us shame. By admitting to ourselves and to God who we really are, we are rebuking the enemy. Telling the enemy that God already knows exactly who we are, where our weaknesses are, and that He still loves us prevents any enemy from gaining a foothold in our lives.

One of the greatest weapons we have against the enemy is being honest and admitting the weaknesses in our lives. The Bible tells us that if God is for us, who can be against us? We also have the promise that there is nothing in this world that can separate us from God's unconditional love (see Rom. 8:31-39).

Who you are when you lay your head on your pillow at night is the real you. It's not the masked person you show the world. If we are really honest with ourselves, we have to admit we pretend a lot. We're strong mothers or fathers, we're strong husbands or wives, we're strong Christian men or women, and we're going to do something positive with our lives. There's nothing wrong with setting those kinds of goals, but at the same time, we must be willing to admit what is really going on inside as we work to attain those goals.

It's at night when we lay our head on the pillow, that the tears and the questions come. When everything is quiet and we can't drown out the pain with busyness and performance, we begin to cry out, "God, where are You? I'm confused, what's going on?" David shows us in the Psalms that it is all right to be honest with our heavenly Father.

Jesus said that God the Father sent Him to heal the brokenhearted and set free those who were oppressed or being held prisoner by the enemy. Jesus personally knows the struggle we face in trying to do the will of the Father and prevent the enemy from getting a foothold in our minds. But He also told us He overcame these things for us.

As a matter of fact, before it was time for Jesus to return to the Father, He told His disciples He had equipped them to go and continue His work. "You will do what I did," He told them, "and even greater works than these will you do" (see John 14:12). This means we are to bring healing to the brokenhearted and freedom to those oppressed and bound by any type of illness. The Church can do this as it is guided by the Great Physician.

Surgery, Not a Band-Aid

In centuries passed, church was looked upon as a sanctuary or safe place where refuge and help could be found. In recent times it seems the Church has offered only a small Band-Aid remedy for what has become a very serious issue among Christians. This lack of proper treatment has left many walking around hurt, wounded, and bleeding inside. How many of us go to God and express our inner turmoil as honestly as David in Psalm 142?

> *I cry out to the Lord; I plead for the Lord's mercy. I pour out my complaints before Him and tell Him all my troubles. When I am overwhelmed, You alone know the way I should turn. Wherever I go, my enemies have set traps for me.* **I look for someone to come and help me, but no one gives me a passing thought! No one will help me; no one cares a bit what happens to me.** *Then I pray to You, O Lord. I say, "You are my place of refuge. You*

are all I really want in life. Hear my cry, for I am very low. Rescue me from my persecutors, for they are too strong for me. Bring me out of prison so I can thank You" (Psalm 142:1-7 NLT).

As disciples of Jesus, our desire is to be prepared to minister to the brokenhearted. Our churches are filled with broken, hurting people who are confused, condemned, and defeated by everything and everyone around them. They feel no one really cares what happens to them. The Church, the Body of Christ, should be a place of safety and refuge, a sanctuary of peace, a place where they can get the help that they need. Unfortunately, the Church has not learned what to do with people when their lives fall apart and they continue to struggle emotionally beyond what is considered a "timely manner." Unable to rationalize their suffering, the tendency is to think it's their fault because they don't have the faith or believe strongly enough for their healing. So even in the Church the afflicted have felt that no one is there to help them.

We tend to put Band-Aids on bleeders and then send them back out into the world telling them to be strong in the Lord and that the joy of the Lord will be their strength. To truly minister to the brokenhearted as instructed by Jesus, we need to understand that these people are deeply wounded and that there are issues deep down in their hearts that need to be dealt with. The only way for the healing to begin is to lance the wound and then do major surgery in the area of infection. As with any major surgery done in the physical realm, there is a recovery time required. The same is true in the spiritual realm.

We may be called to stand alongside these fellow Christians for more than one session of prayer. We may need to hold their hand as the Lord lances the wound and does the surgery needed to bring them to wholeness. We may need to encourage them through a time of recovery and rehabilitation. When somebody breaks a leg, everyone expects to see a cast on that leg and understands there is a recovery time and physical therapy needed to help the leg regain strength and function properly again. God's healing works in a similar way. I believe the Church should function as an emergency room, an operating room, a recovery room, and a rehabilitation center for those wounded in soul and spirit.

Answers, Not Clichés

I searched deeply trying to understand what happened and why I was unable to live victoriously in Christ. Even though I thought Christians were not supposed to struggle emotionally or spiritually, I was fighting for my life. I looked to the Church and seasoned believers but the answers and advice I received were often hollow and full of clichés.

I came face to face with questions like: Maybe God isn't who He says He is? Who is He anyway? Maybe Christianity isn't the way to God? Perhaps I have built my life on lies? Why was I born? What is life really all about? Though these questions haunted me daily, I knew deep within my heart that God was the answer to my problem. I was certain that the world's solutions offered me no hope at all, but I didn't seem to be able to find a way to recover in body, soul, and spirit.

I existed in the many stages of depression, despair, anxiety, and fear, and I continued to cry out to God. As I blindly stumbled around hoping to find a place of peace and rest, I became more and more overwhelmed by the daily routines of life. I tried to find comfort and safety in the shelter of family, friends, and activities. When that no longer worked, I retreated into isolation to avoid people and the ever-increasing pressures of life and ministry. No matter what I tried, I could not escape my inner anxiety and pain.

I witnessed a prayer session where Chrystal made a choice to feel the deep pain and sadness and wait for the Lord to bring her what she needed to know about that time in her life. Chrystal was able to embrace the pain and let the Lord bring her through with hope, healing, and a sense of real joy.[4]

Since then I have come to realize that we hide when we hurt because we don't understand the healing offered through Christ. We really don't comprehend that when God heals, He also transforms every part of us: body, soul, and spirit. We become discouraged when the process we must walk through takes more than one prayer or one counseling session. The Church must become better equipped to deal with this epidemic of depression and brokenness that is permeating the Body of Christ.

The Bible provides us with a framework that takes into account the most current scientific findings from which we can understand depression, its multiple causes, its varying degrees of intensity and course, as well as its critical spiritual dimensions. From this framework spiritual, psychological, social, physiological and medical interventions are possible.[5]

Dealing With Depression

Unfortunately, in our zeal to bring healing to the depressed, Christians have often unwittingly done things that torment rather than treat depressed people. We need to learn what *not* to do as well as what *can* be done to complement whatever professional treatment may be prescribed. In order to deal with depression effectively, we need to study what depression really is, what the potential causes might be, and how to be an effective part of the treatment.

Depression is by far the most common form of mental suffering. It is, however, a poorly defined condition that means different things to different people. We must be able to distinguish between the discouragement of a recent disappointment and the severe crushing despair that is characteristic of depression. Depression is both physical and psychosomatic; but however psychosomatically it may have been induced, depression is a very real physical condition.

> Depression is one of the most common health conditions in the world. Depression isn't a weakness, nor is it something that you can simply "snap out of." Depression, formally called major depression, major depressive disorder or clinical depression, is a medical illness that involves the mind and body. It affects how you think and behave and can cause a variety of emotional and physical problems. You may not be able to go about your usual daily activities, and depression may make you feel as if life just isn't worth living anymore. Most health professionals today consider depression a chronic illness that requires long-term treatment, much like diabetes or high blood pressure. Although some people experience only one episode of depression, most have repeated episodes of depression symptoms throughout their life. Effective diagnosis and treatment can help reduce even severe depression symptoms. And with effective treatment, most people with depression feel better, often within weeks, and can return to the daily activities they previously enjoyed.[6]

In short, "depression is a condition in which our personal spirit has died to its capacity to sustain the person fully, either emotionally or physically."[7] In depression a person's spirit struggles desperately to sustain the physical body, often failing to sustain the psychological state of the individual. The depressed have little or no energy to perform even simple functions and have no capacity to feel joy, contentment, or hope.

The most telling characteristic of a depressed person is *despair*. Depressed individuals are not only without hope; they know for a fact that tomorrow won't be any better than today. Their candle of hope has been totally extinguished, leaving them trying to exist in a life void of joy and surrounded only by darkness. They have been robbed of even the simple pleasures of life and wonder why no one is trying to help them find their way out of the oppressive darkness all around them.

Many people have experienced depression at least once in their life. The predominant effect of depression is a loss of energy where a person finds there are few if any motivations in life. Although this feels terrible, people in the midst of such depression are still able to accomplish what they need to do in order to survive. They go to work, pay the bills, cook their meals, and relate to the people in their life who demand their attention. This type of depression feels rotten, but life continues in spite of it. These individuals continue to function but fail to thrive.

Major Depression

Major depression is experienced when that despair invades every part of your life. Every experience feels like a failure or is too frustrating to even attempt. Eventually, you try to avoid as many experiences as possible, dwindling your daily sphere of activity down to virtually nothing. You have no sense that your doom or gloom will ever disappear. In a major depression, the symptoms are much more severe, last much longer, and eventually impair a person's ability to function. These individuals fail to function and fail to thrive.

Major depression is clinically defined (DSM-III-R) through the evaluation of several criteria. To be diagnosed as having major depression, a person must exhibit at least five of the following nine symptoms pretty much daily for at least two weeks:

1. Depressed mood most of the day.

2. Diminished interest or pleasure in almost all activities of the day.

3. Significant weight gain or loss and decreased appetite.

4. Insomnia or hypersomnia (too much sleeping).

5. Abnormal restlessness or a drop in physical activity.

6. Fatigue or loss of energy.

7. Feelings of worthlessness or excessive or inappropriate guilt.

8. Diminished ability to think, concentrate, or make decisions.

9. Recurrent thoughts of death or suicidal without a specific plan; or a suicide attempt; or a specific plan for committing suicide.

These symptoms must reflect a change from that person's ordinary behavior and are not caused by another illness or the loss of a loved one. We all have times of disappointment and grief, as well as times of elation and ecstasy. In a normal person, the overall balance is that of being relaxed, content, feeling in control, concentrating normally, being clear-headed, and coping with stresses.

Science tells us that there are very specific chemical substances called *neurotransmitters* that are produced by our brains to regulate our moods. If anything happens to disrupt the production of these chemicals, then the control center will malfunction and mood will fluctuate outside of normal range and we lose the ability to control our thoughts. The cause of this imbalance is twofold: stress or trauma and genetic makeup.

Emotional Health

Depression overshadows and consumes our emotional state, causing us to feel extremely negative about ourselves, our lives, and our future. Emotions are one of the three fundamental God-given building blocks of our personalities. The other two are intelligence and will. To function at the level of wholeness that God intends for us, we must be healthy in all three of these areas. Our measure of fulfillment in life is directly related to and dependent on our emotional health, whether we want to admit it or not.

The Christian community and society in general have been reluctant to address emotional issues that so many believers struggle with their whole lives. The Church in general prefers not to discuss or think about emotional issues, mainly because they don't have any idea what to do with damaged emotions. The Church either avoids the issue or places blame on the individual, concluding it is their weakness that keeps them depressed. This causes shame to enter the picture and pushes the hurting believer even farther down into the pit of depression and despair.

I have discovered that many in the Body of Christ assume that at the moment of salvation everything is fixed and we can press on in victory. Therefore any believer who stumbles along the way is dismissed as weak, undisciplined, poorly motivated, disobedient, and carnal. This attitude causes Christians to deny their emotional battles, sweep them under the rug, and believe that if they were a stronger Christian they could overcome these problems. This mindset produces more defeat and disillusionment in the already wounded Christian.

The truth is, God desires to deal with our emotional baggage by removing the hurt and pain from our lives, not denying its existence. Since depression is caused by either a genetic chemical imbalance or through a stress- or trauma-induced chemical imbalance, there is a multistep process we must go through to begin the journey to recovery and victory.

Whether you are walking this journey yourself or are coming alongside a fellow Christian, the steps are the same.

1. Acceptance Step: Honestly accept where you are.

2. Question Step: Do I really want to be healed and set free? Will I allow God to do this healing in His way and time?

3. Patience Step: Be patient with yourself and with what you observe God doing in you.

4. Nurturing Step: Realize both your physical and spiritual health are in need of nurturing.

Manic Depressive Illness

Bipolar disorder or manic depressive illness affects about 2 percent of the population and is commonly thought to begin in a person's teens, twenties, or thirties. Both men and women suffer from the disease, and some research indicates that the illness is hereditary. Sufferers experience depression lasting between three and six months, along with at least one episode of mania or lesser degrees of excitement.

There are different forms that this disease can take and diagnosis is based upon a distinctive pattern of symptoms. About one in three people with bipolar disease can experience both depression and mania simultaneously. Although admission to the hospital may be necessary, except for severe forms of the disease, medication and therapy are helpful in treating the disorder. Although when the individual experiences flare-ups, bipolar disease may appear to be overwhelming; the prognosis for most patients is very good. Most people diagnosed with bipolar disease are eventually able to resume normal activities.[8]

I experienced depression and was eventually diagnosed with bipolar illness. I experienced firsthand the effects of mental illness on my physical, emotional, and spiritual health. I also had to deal with the wrong mind-set concerning the cause and treatment of mental illness. By sharing what I have walked through and learned about depression and mental illness, I hope to help other Christians find the kind of help they really need to overcome and attain victory in their lives. The next chapter will give some specifics on the type of ministry we have developed to make the Church a safe place for those who struggle emotionally.

I met Chrystal while attending a seminar at LWCC. When I heard her testimony about being diagnosed as bipolar and how God healed her, it gave me hope that I too could receive the kind of help I needed to deal with my mental disorder. A lot of people I've talked with about my disorder don't understand how to guide someone along the path to healing. The very first session I had with Chrystal and her assistant showed me they would not judge or condemn me. In fact I felt they were really taking an interest in me and were in this with me to see it through to the end. They made me feel relaxed and comfortable and that my personal safety was of the utmost importance as I journey through to wholeness. They actually paid attention to what I was saying and responded with compassion and encouragement showing me they truly had my best interest at heart. For the first time in my life I felt I was worth something to someone and they were willing to invest time in me for the long haul.[9]

My Adventure and Journey With God

1. Who are you when you lay your head on your pillow at night? Are you filled with questions, sorrows, and despair or are you at rest and peace?

2. Have you gone to God and expressed your inner turmoil as honestly as David did in Psalm 142:1-7? If not, take the time right now to do so. Personalize this Psalm by putting your name in the blanks and then use it as your prayer.

I [_____] *cry out to the Lord; I* [_____] *plead for the Lord's mercy. I* [_____] *pour out my complaints before Him and tell Him all my troubles. When I* [_____] *am overwhelmed, You alone know the way I should turn. Wherever I* [_____] *go, my enemies have set traps for me. I* [_____] **look for someone to come and help me, but no one gives me a passing thought! No one will help me; no one cares a bit what happens to me.** *Then I* [_____] *pray to You, O Lord. I say, "You are my place of refuge. You are all I really want in life. Hear my cry, for I am very low. Rescue me* [_____] *from my persecutors, for they are too strong for me. Bring me* [_____] *out of prison so I can thank You"* (Psalm 142:1-7 NLT).

3. What have you learned about depression and the role of the Body of Christ?

4. In what ways has the Church put Band-Aids on this serious issue? What will you do differently now in dealing with someone who may be experiencing some form of mental illness?

CHAPTER 11

A MINISTRY OF
TRANSFORMATION

MY LIFE MESSAGE AND PASSION is creating moments for individuals to experience the miraculous transforming power of Christ so they can fully live as Christ designed. When I see the overall lack of victory, power, and peace displayed in the Body of Christ, I'm compelled to share what I have learned from my personal journey with mental illness. Though not every believer experiences the depth of struggle I endured, everyone is acquainted with their own overwhelming emotions, unanswered questions, and unexpected circumstances.

Every believer has heard that God is our shield and victory and that we are supposed to have the joy of the Lord deep in our hearts. However, far too many live outside the promises of the Scriptures, struggling to show the appearance of victory. I remember what it was like to ask myself on a regular basis, *What's wrong with me that I can't live the joyous, victorious life?* I know that the answer only lies in a God who promised to bring us into the full measure of Christ through renewing and transforming the heart and lives of all who would call upon Him.

> I believe that what Chrystal and her team are doing with this ministry is beyond words. Fantastic, phenomenal, super… those words just don't even come close to expressing how blessed I've been by participating in a ministry of transformation called Kairos. My life has been changed forever by what I've experienced… I can't think of any one word that describes my gratitude. Chrystal has chosen to make a stand in an arena where people are so desperately in need of healing. People in the Church need healing, people outside of church need healing, people around the globe need healing. I have been so blessed by Chrystal's compassion and passion to see people healed. I pray that God takes this ministry and Chrystal's testimony to places beyond our wildest expectations![1]

A Ministry of Transformation

Kairos[2] is a ministry of transformation. It is an entire program that we've developed to help believers grow and live in the transforming power of Christ as it is expressed in Isaiah 61:1-4. We offer classes that share the biblical principles I learned through my personal journey and struggles. We create a safe place for one-on-one prayer sessions to occur and a place where people discuss and share things they've never been able to tell anybody before.

We offer help to those who are suffering, confused, disappointed, broken, hurt, lost, and searching for answers, as well as those dealing with addiction, sexual abuse, divorce, and any other life issue. We show believers that God wants to restore them, renew them, and bring them back to life. We show them that the very thing that the enemy sought to use to destroy them becomes the sword they will use to set somebody else free.

> I was part of the prayer team ministry when Chrystal and Ken first came to Living Water. She and Ken were people I prayed for on a regular basis. Everything hit the fan shortly after the birth of her third child. I was not aware of the gravity of her illness until one Sunday when Pastor Ken shared with the congregation the fact that he would not be as available to us because he needed to be there for his wife. Again my job was to pray. I remember at one point in my prayer time the Lord had given me a word for Chrystal. It was that God had counted her worthy to go through this season because He had great things He wanted her to do. After the healing it was as God had said—He was using her to help heal the brokenhearted He was bringing into her life and into the church. I know that God used Chrystal's challenges so that she would be able to reach the hurting. I am impressed how God has been able to take these challenges and develop a ministry to heal broken people. I remember that when she first started the ministry she felt overwhelmed with the sea of humanity that was hurting. She surrounded herself with strong people, but the need was great and the resources were minimal. God has done a great work to give her clarity of vision and insight to realize that to reach the multitudes you have to develop systems. I feel privileged to have been able to be there in Chrystal's time of need if only to be a behind-the-scenes prayer partner.[3]

Testimonies

The ministry that Chrystal is now head of came out of her illness, but it is more than just helping people who suffer from mental illness. I am an adult who was recovering from being raped and sexually abused as a child, and because of this ministry I have been emotionally healed of a lot of things, especially my anger. I have now been able to help other women who have gone through a similar fate. One of the purposes of this ministry is to help people move from brokenness to wholeness, and I am so excited for what Chrystal has done through her own life experience with mental illness. She didn't just deal with the mental illness issues, she branched into many areas where people are not living victorious lives. I have seen many people helped through so many areas of life when nothing else they did worked.[4]

One night in the Kairos 3 class, Pastor Paulette Horvath, Associate Pastor of Transformation, was demonstrating how to conduct a prayer session, and I had volunteered to be the one prayed for. I had planned on discussing an issue that was pretty close to the surface and not too emotionally charged. Well, God showed up in that moment and changed all my plans! I started to relinquish some very painful events in my life that I never thought I'd share with a group...let alone with a group containing men. But it was at that moment of brutal honesty that I physically felt a shift in my heart. I knew in an instant that God had broken the bondage of secrecy off of me. God showed me that I don't need to hide the truth of my life from others. I had to do that all my life but no more. As an adult, I can choose when to share and trust God that my story will be a blessing to someone else who may be struggling. Without this class and this ministry, I don't know that this would be my reality today.[5]

I've got a master's in psychology and am currently interning for my CADC (Certified Alcohol and Drug Addiction Counselor). I've also taken a workshop that focused on the desire Christ has to heal. But my greatest identification was to the "spiritual" wounding Chrystal described as a result of her father's death just before her birth and grandfather's death. You see, I was conceived out of wedlock in the late 1950s to Roman Catholic German and Irish parents who married largely because of my sudden unexpected arrival in the womb. This was a HUGE secret in my family, shared ONLY with me by my mother about 15 years ago. My mother revealed to me the horror, shame, and lies surrounding the pregnancy and the rushed wedding. I was a fail-to-thrive infant, fragile, sickly, and allergic to my mother's milk. All of my young and adult life found me feeling "different," inadequate, flawed, shameful, and thinking that there was some horrible unspoken secret about me that doomed my success, peace, and joy. I've since completed all three levels and am now an intern in the Kairos Ministry. I've experienced God's presence and work of transformation personally and have identified sources of my continued struggles in emotions, thoughts, and behavior rooted in generational and personal sin and spiritual wounds. I continue to receive blessings as I'm ministered to and in my ministry internship.[6]

Redemptive Suffering

One of the first areas we deal with in this ministry is the subject of suffering. There are many questions and a lot of misunderstanding when we as Christians are in the midst of suffering. Many times we pray and ask God to deliver us out of our wilderness times, but there is usually something God wants us to learn before He does that. If we can at least acknowledge that the Lord is accomplishing something in our lives, we can determine to cooperate with Him until we can see the light at the end of the tunnel. Even during some of my darkest hours I would pray, "God, I want to cooperate with whatever You're doing in my life. Even though I don't understand it and I'm angry with You, please don't take this from me until You have accomplished Your will" (see John 13:7; Proverbs 20:24; Ecclesiastes 7:13).

Suffering is redemptive when we allow the Lord to do what He wants to do and not just pray for a quick rescue. If we would begin to ask the right questions, then our suffering can become redemptive. "God, what are You doing in my life? What are You after in me?" When we allow the Lord to show us what He's doing in and through us, His strength is made available as we walk through our times of suffering.

It takes a lot of determination to allow our trials and situations to produce good fruit rather than negative attitudes. The Bible says we are to consider it joy as we face trials in life and learn to persevere. When we do so, God promises us that we will be "complete" and "lack nothing" (see James 1:2-4). The apostle Paul understood this concept when he explained his suffering and his *"thorn in the flesh"* (2 Cor. 12:7). Paul prayed for God to remove it, but when He did not, Paul accepted it as something God allowed to keep Paul from failing in his life destiny.

I had to come to that place as well. I didn't know if the Lord was going to heal me. I didn't know if I was ever even going to recover. I just knew I had to surrender it all to the Lord. I came to a place where I could say, "Lord, if You designate that the rest of my life will be like this, then I'll still give You the glory." We read in Hebrews 11 that some of the heroes of faith did not receive what they believed for and yet they were all commended for their faith. *"Therefore, since we are surrounded by such a great cloud of witnesses,"* Paul says, *"let us throw off everything that hinders* [us]*...and let us run with perseverance the race marked out for us. ...*[Let us] *not grow weary and lose heart"* (Heb. 12:1-3).

I came to the realization that there are people whom God doesn't heal, and my father, Carl, was one of them. I thought perhaps I might also be one of the ones who would not receive a total healing. If that was the case, I had to deal with what my relationship with God was going to be like. If He didn't rescue me, if He didn't heal me, what would my attitude toward Him be? Would I choose to stay on the path of bitterness and wallow in self-pity, or would I trust Him enough to move beyond those negative feelings and try to discover what God was doing in my life?

I made the decision to serve Him no matter what He chose to do. My whole life focus had to change. Instead of focusing on myself and my circumstances, I had to focus on what God was doing and cooperate with Him. I had no expectations of healing yet I never stopped wanting God to heal me. I learned a powerful truth once I set my heart and affections on Him instead of what was happening to me. I found that, *God was more concerned with what I was becoming than what I was doing for Him.*

Why Has God Forsaken Me?

Suffering enters all of our lives at one point or another. It is not an invited guest and is often perceived as an unwanted intruder. In the midst of that intrusion, we experience devastation, confusion, hurt, and pain. We are left wondering what in the world is going on and where God is in all of this. Because suffering is a word that encompasses a broad spectrum of experiences, we need to more clearly define it.

Suffering is any experience where we are forced to endure pain, heart-ache, and distress. In order to understand the concept of redemptive suffering, we also need a definition of redemption. It means to make something worthwhile or offset a bad effect.

Most of us have made an assumption that something is wrong with suffering. We look at suffering as something to avoid, escape, and run away from. We believe we should not have to endure any kind of suffering in our lives once we become Christians. This mind-set is revealed when we ask questions like:

- What is the meaning of my suffering?

- Where does it come from?

- Who causes suffering?

- Is it possible that it is caused by the God who loves me?

- Why doesn't God relieve my pain? He could if He wanted to, couldn't He?

- Isn't the suffering of my life a waste because if I were whole I could be doing so much more for God?

- Why is a loving God allowing this?

- Does every Christian have to go through suffering?

- Isn't He Jehovah Rapha, the Great Physician? Why isn't He healing me?

- Shouldn't it be different for Christians? What is wrong with me? Did I make a mistake that brought on this despair?

Take heart, fellow Christians, because the Psalmist David asked some very similar questions in the midst of his sufferings:

My God, my God, why have You forsaken me? Why are You so far from saving me, so far from the words of my groaning? (Psalm 22:1)

How long, O Lord? Will You forget me forever? How long will You hide Your face from me? How long must I wrestle with my thoughts and every day have sorrow in my heart? (Psalm 13:1-2)

Why, O Lord, do You stand far off? Why do You hide Yourself in times of trouble? (Psalm 10:1)

Christians hold many beliefs about the cause of suffering. One belief is that we have somehow failed God. We believe we must have done something terribly wrong or we wouldn't be experiencing such suffering. Some people reason that suffering exists so God can do a miracle at a later time. We refer to the story of Hannah, where God closed her womb so that one day He might miraculously open it and she would conceive the prophet Samuel (see I Samuel 1). We read how one day the disciples asked Jesus whose sin was responsible for the man born blind. Jesus replied that it happened so that the Son of God could be glorified (see John 9:1-3). Others believe that their lack of faith has impaired their ability to receive healing, so they ask questions like: How do I know if I have faith? How do I get it? How big is a mustard seed in regard to faith?

Any one of these could be a possible explanation of someone's suffering. We suffer when we sin because the wages of sin is death. It is also true that God desires to relieve pain and suffering and do the miraculous among us for His glory. Faith is part of the healing process. There are those who don't believe the truth and so their suffering and pain continues. I believe that though pain is unpleasant, there is another way of looking at suffering.

The Crucible of Suffering

There are times in our lives where suffering is a necessary part of a growth process rather than something to avoid at all cost. I have learned that we *cannot* enter into our personal destiny in God unless we allow ourselves to be changed into His likeness. I believe almost everyone would agree with me that change is not easy and often causes a level of suffering along the way. As a matter of fact, the process of this transformation in God is often wrought in the crucible of suffering.

Throughout the pages of Scripture, suffering can be seen as a tool God uses to transform His children into His likeness. It can be seen as the way to life, the way to experience life, and the way to understand life. Suffering can be seen as something that opens the door to the very heart of God. But we must understand that God is not the author of suffering, He uses it to fulfill His purposes.

I realize that this is a hard truth to digest and believe. If we are going to get to the place where we can accept that suffering is a tool used by God to bring transformation to our lives, we must first understand something about the way God thinks. Until we gain a measure of understanding here, we will continue to view our suffering as something that is bad and that God ought to take away—immediately.

How God sees things is often opposite from how we see things. He tells us this in Isaiah 55:9 (NLT), *"My ways are higher than your ways and My thoughts higher than your thoughts."* In other words if we have a differing view than God's, let's not waste time determining who is right or wrong, or whose way is better. Second Samuel 22:31 states, *"As for God, His way is perfect."* We can't outdo perfect.

Scripture also reveals to us that His ways are full of paradoxes:

- To be first, you become last (see Matthew 20:16).

- To be strong, you become weak (see 2 Corinthians 12:10).

- The foolish are wise (see I Corinthians 1:20-28).

- You lose your life to find it (see Matthew 16:25).

- Giving is receiving (see Luke 6:38).

- The least in the Kingdom is the greatest (see Matthew 18:4).

James 1:2-4 sounds like an oxymoron; it makes the point that there are times when our suffering leads us to a better place.

> *Consider it **pure** joy, my brothers, whenever you face trials of many kinds, because you know that the testing of your faith develops perseverance. Perseverance must finish its work so that you may be mature and complete, not lacking anything* (James 1:2-4).

Saying yes to God and no to self will mean suffering to one degree or another. But it also means that we are coming closer to the image of God that we were created to be. If we are going to do anything significant for God, we must learn to submit life to the processes of God. If the crucible of suffering is used to bring transformation, then we must embrace that as the way God is purifying us. So how do we do that? How should we look at this crucible of suffering? How can this crucible of suffering have redemption packaged into it?

The Four D's of Transformation

This process of transformation through suffering has four elements and is a recurring event in our lives. Each time we enter the process we should be experiencing it on a deeper level than the time before. The problem is that many of us repeat the cycle without ever going deeper.

By learning the four elements of this transformation process, we can better cooperate with God's purposes for us.

First of all, God will make specific *declarations* stating His purposes and plans for our lives. In order for us to reach that God-ordained destiny, He must work in our hearts to get everything out of us that should not be there. God deals with every hindrance in us, and this is where we are often plunged into suffering and times of *distress* and pain. This plunge into the crucible of suffering occurs so that God is able to begin to *develop* us. Distress and development go hand in hand, but sometimes we get so hung up in our distress that we don't allow God to develop us. God uses the trauma of our circumstances to develop us into what we need to be to achieve our destiny.

When our development reaches a point that blesses the Lord, then there is the final element of the process: the *demonstration of our destiny*, all that God has said He would do. He fulfills all the promises He has made to us, and we begin to function as He has designed us.

Joseph

In Genesis, chapters 37, 39-45, we read the story of a young man named Joseph. He became a true man of God because he yielded himself to the ways of God. Joseph was personally transformed so he could be effective for God no matter what the situation or circumstance he encountered in his life.

We see the *declaration* of God's purposes for Joseph through two dreams he had as a young man. When declarations or decrees of the Lord are made, they rarely come to pass immediately because there is a process involved in their unfolding and fulfillment. Joseph was not ready to walk into a position of leadership at the moment he received those dreams. He did not even have sense enough to keep his mouth shut concerning his dreams, which caused strife and jealousy in his relationships with the rest of his family. He was immature and needed development before he could ever walk in the promise of the dreams he had received. God had to make Joseph's life fit the decree and declarations he had received.

How many of us believe the promises or prophetic words of God and embrace them until we encounter situations that are the exact opposite of what God has declared? I knew God had called me into full-time ministry, so I did everything I could to attain that goal. But when I started having anxiety attacks and unexplainable highs and lows, I began to question the promises.

Joseph gets this word from God about ruling and reigning. Next he is thrown into a deep dark hole and sold into slavery by his own brothers. His life went in the opposite direction of the declaration God made over his life. Instead of ruling he become a slave. I believe it is safe to say that Joseph was probably experiencing some distress. Wouldn't you be? It was in this crucible of *distress, despair,* and suffering that God developed and transformed Joseph into the man he would need to be in order to walk out his destiny in God.

A divine contradiction takes place. God speaks the promises and prophecies of our destiny, then He takes us down before He brings us up. As a matter of fact, God often takes us into places where nobody wants to know us or even be with us because this crucible is about building a relationship with Him that will last a lifetime. We must embrace first the place where God means more than anything else in life—more than the promises or gifting, more than our ministry, and more than His hand of blessing.

This can be a major hurdle for many of us. We desire the fulfillment of blessings promised, the answers, the relief, the deliverance, the healing, and the ministry more than the relationship with Him. If we don't understand what God is doing, we will fight against this place God has taken us. Just as the Scripture says, Israel knew the acts of God, but Moses knew His ways (see Psalm 103:7). So God is so merciful that He allows us to walk through this place as many times as needed. He desires for us to know His ways, not just His acts. We often refer to this as taking another lap around the mountain. He only allows that and is patient with us because He knows how important this truth is to our development. How many times we have to repeat the walk is up to us, and is often determined by how we handle this crucible of suffering.

Joseph went from the *declaration* to the *distress* part of God's transformation process. God uses Joseph's time as a slave in Potiphar's house and then as a prisoner in an Egyptian jail to *develop* the skills necessary to fulfill the role He has in mind for Joseph to play. Joseph was learning to trust God in every circumstance. The distress and development stages are interwoven to produce trust in us in two very crucial ways.

Every day we are learning to trust the Lord for our finances, our health, and everything we need for life. The only way I was able to survive my time in the pit of depression was to develop an unshakable trust in the Lord. Only one way exists to overcome anxiety, panic, and depression, and that is to trust that God loves you and means it when He says, *"I will never leave you nor forsake you"* (Josh. 1:5; see also Heb. 13:5).

Then we must develop to a place where God can trust us. We must be careful in this place not to fall into the trap of murmuring and complaining. We cannot allow our circumstances to take us away from God. If all we want is to be rescued from our distress, we will remain unchanged and unfit for the destiny God has placed before us. This distress and development phase of transformation is designed by God to bring us into a closer relationship with Him where we trust Him even when we cannot see where we are going.

Hebrews 10:23 says, *"Let us hold unswervingly to the hope we profess, for He who promised is faithful."* Then in verse 36 it says, *"You need to persevere so that when you have done the will of God, you will receive what He has promised."* I had to get to the place where I could honestly tell God, "Even if You never heal me, I will continue to serve You to the best of my ability."

In the process of distress and development in Joseph's life, God formed and fashioned him into the man that he needed to be in order to fulfill the dreams given him in his youth. When God determined Joseph was ready, He elevated Joseph to a place where he would rule and reign as second in command to Pharaoh.

The crucible of suffering is where God deals with all the things in us that shouldn't be there. It is the place where God prepares us for the good works He destined us for and where the demonstration of what has been promised can be fulfilled. Suffering can be redemptive if we allow it to be. We can choose to participate with God and cooperate with His process or we can try to find our own way out and remain slaves to our circumstances.

> I've been taking the Kairos classes for the past three years and I've gained so much from each class! These truly were life-changing moments for me. After they happened, I knew my life would never be the same. I have no idea where God is taking me on this journey, but I do know for certain that there has been a passion ignited in my heart to see people healed due to the Kairos ministry. I now have a desire to see people walking in forgiveness, love, and pure joy every day of their lives. Kairos has been instrumental in allowing me to

see firsthand what healing looks like on the faces of others. I was so wounded when I was receiving ministry that I could not think outside of myself. But once I stepped into the Kairos classes, all of that changed![7]

"Thorns and Thrones"

I'd rather gather roses
without thorns, Lord,
A bright and fragrant,
beautiful bouquet
To decorate my world
with pretty pleasures-
The brambles and the briers,
I'll throw away.
But you say I must pluck
the thorns as well, Lord,
Though they'll pierce my heart
and sting my soul;
You say that pain's
a part of peace, you tell me
That breaking is a part
of being whole....
You say that if I truly
want to know you,
I must count everything
but Christ a loss;
You ask me to exchange my will
for yours, Lord,
To trade contentment's kingdom
for a cross.

And so I come before you,
weak but willing;
I seek to walk your path,
and not my own;
I choose to share
the crown of thorns
you wore, Lord,
Until I kneel before
your royal throne.

—B.J. Hoff[8]

My Adventure and Journey With God

1. Read again "Thorns and Thrones." What areas of your heart and life do you need to lie down and surrender?

2. What stage of transformation do you see yourself in, and why? Have you had to spend some time in the crucible of suffering?

3. Personalize the following Scriptures by putting your name in the blanks.

"For I know the plans I have for you, [_____]," *declares the Lord, "plans to prosper you* [_____]
and not to harm you [_____], *plans to give you* [_____] *hope and a future"*
(Jeremiah 29:11).

*Being confident of this, that He who began a good work in you
[_____] will carry it on to completion un-
til the day of Christ Jesus* (Philippians 1:6).

*For it is God who works in you [_____] to will
and to act according to His good purpose* (Philippians 2:13).

4. Have you received a specific word or prophecy spoken over
   your life? Write that word here and continue to believe in
   what He has spoken and declared over you. Read Psalms
   119:49, 138:2b; 33:4.

   _____

   _____

   _____

   _____

5. What have you learned from this chapter in dealing with
   your suffering? Can you view your crucible of suffering in
   a redemptive way?

6. When you can, offer this prayer to the Lord in the midst of
   your suffering or difficult circumstance:

   Heavenly Father, I pray You accomplish all You desire in
   my heart and life through every circumstance I face. I say
   to You what Mary said in Luke 1:38 (KJV) *"...be it unto me
   according to your word."*

CHAPTER 12

DON'T JUST SURVIVE; *THRIVE!*

To *SURVIVE* MEANS TO ENDURE or live through an affliction or adversity. Surviving means you have managed to stay alive against overwhelming odds. We have heard people say they've survived a plane crash or survived cancer. To *thrive* means to grow or develop vigorously; to flourish, to prosper or be successful. For example, as parents our heart's desire for our children is that they not only survive in this world but that they truly thrive. God's heart is the same for us as His children.

In John 10:9-10, Jesus explained the reason the Father sent Him:

I am the Gate. Anyone who goes through Me will be cared for—will freely go in and out, and find pasture. A thief is only there to steal and kill and destroy. I came so they can have real and eternal life, more and better life than they ever dreamed of (John 10:9-10 TM).

The New Living Translation says:

My purpose is to give them a rich and satisfying life (John 10:10b NLT).

The Amplified Bible says it still another way:

The thief comes only in order to steal and kill and destroy. I came that they may have and enjoy life, and have it in abundance (to the full, till it overflows) (John 10:10 AMP).

God desires for us to thrive, to live, to grow, and to flourish by being connected with who we are, with Him, and with each other. I have discovered that if we are struggling and not thriving, there is a disconnection in one of these three areas. We can either keep trying to push through like we've been doing, barely surviving and unfulfilled, or we can connect as God designed and thrive. Jesus shows us the way, but we have to choose to walk in His ways.

Adam and Eve

In Genesis, chapters 1 and 2, God created the first two people, blessed them, and gave them a job to do. In the Garden of Eden, Adam and Eve are in a life-giving relationship with God, each other, and creation. God gave them a choice to be obedient to His commands. He warned them not to eat from the tree of life or they would die.

When Adam and Eve chose to disobey God's command, a disconnect occurred between them and God, between the woman and the man, and between man and creation. We are born into a world that has existed in this continued state, both physically and relationally. We feel dissatisfied with life, unfulfilled in our relationships, and many feel lost and passionless. All this has left us asking: Is this all there is? Will my life only amount to this?

Survival is simply pushing through life using our own devices. We may choose to pursue career advancements and education only to find we still feel empty, void, and unfulfilled. We find a mate and marry, only to live separate lives, pursuing different goals and passions, leaving us empty and alone in our marital relationship. We look in the mirror and wonder who is staring back at us. We appear to be living but on the inside we are dying a slow death.

Reconnected With Ourselves

When Adam and Eve chose to disobey God in the Garden, guilt and shame entered into human history. We now look in the mirror haunted by our physical flaws so we develop masks to hide them. We learn to deny who we really are, thinking we are undeserving, and we search for and long for attention and affirmation. The masks we wear erode and suppress our personalities to the point that we are in danger of losing our true selves.

This disconnection with ourselves becomes a stumbling block in our relationships with others and God. I would shrink back from relating because of how I felt about myself. Jesus told His disciples that we are to love our neighbor as we love ourselves (see Matthew 22:39). He also said the world would know we are His disciples by how we love one another (see John 13:35). If we can't love ourselves, we cannot fulfill these instructions.

The way of overcoming this discontent with ourselves and reconnecting with who we really are is to embrace the truth of what God says about us. Psalm 139:14 gives us a perfect way to pray and thank

God for how He has made us: *"I praise You because I am fearfully and wonderfully made; Your works are wonderful, I know that full well."* In other words, God did not make a mistake when He made you and me. We each need to grasp this powerful truth so we can move ahead and become all that God has called us to be.

Reconnection With God

Adam and Eve became disconnected from God because they believed the lie of the enemy and felt God was withholding something from them. Even though we might not say it out loud, we often feel God is withholding good from us and we believe we know a better way than God's way. We may also hide from God, as Adam and Eve did. Filled with shame, we hide from the wrong choices, not wanting Him to see that we have chosen our own way.

Jesus became the bridge for us to reconnect to God. In Matthew 18:2-5, Jesus told us how to reconnect with our heavenly Father.

> *For an answer Jesus called over a child, whom He stood in the middle of the room, and said, "I'm telling you, once and for all, that unless you return to square one and start over like children, you're not even going to get a look at the kingdom, let alone get in. Whoever becomes simple and elemental again, like this child, will rank high in God's kingdom"* (Matthew 18:2-5 TM).

It's the childlike trust, innocence, and dependence that brings a connection with our Father. In John 14:6, Jesus said, *"I am the Way and the Truth and the Life; no one comes to the Father except by (through) Me"* (John 14:6 AMP).

Reconnecting With Each Other

When Adam and Eve ate of the tree and were confronted by God about what happened, they played the first round of the blame game. Adam blamed God for giving him a defective mate. Eve then blamed the serpent for deceiving her. The blame game always builds walls between individuals. When we feel we have to hide a part of who we are from others, we will remain disconnected from them. This disconnection comes from hiding parts of ourselves and never allowing others into the deepest places of our thoughts and struggles.

To tear down those walls, we must have those we can talk to about everything we are experiencing. Hurt, unresolved anger, false expectations, and failures have to be dug up and dealt with before we can reconnect with others. The problem is that the more exposed we are, the more it hurts; and when we allow others in, we increase the risk of additional hurt (see James 5:16).

Afraid that God would no longer be able to love me if I was unlovable, I feared letting others see me and gain a glimpse into the deepest part of my soul, fearing I would not be loved and accepted—especially in Christian circles. The alternative was to shut down and build a protective wall around my heart while my relationship with others slowly died.

Jesus explained the importance of our relationships with others in John 15:11 (TM):

> I've told you these things for a purpose: that My joy might be your joy, and your joy wholly mature. This is My command: Love one another the way I loved you. This is the very best way to love. Put your life on the line for your friends. You are My friends when you do the things I command you.

God's Divine Power

God desires for us to thrive. We can only reach that level of life by being connected with ourselves, with Him, and with each other. He has shown us the way to accomplish a life far superior to that of just survival. As we conclude this chapter, let's study this powerful passage:

> For **His divine power** has bestowed upon us **all** things that [are requisite and suited] to life and godliness, through the [full, personal] knowledge of Him Who called us by and to His own glory and excellence (virtue) (2 Peter 1:3 AMP).

Jesus has restored us to a right relationship with God through His death and resurrection. Jesus told us that He is the Way, the Truth, and the Life and that no one can come to the Father except through Him. Once that relationship is restored and we are reconnected with God through Jesus, we tap into the divine power that provides us with everything we need to thrive.

> By means of these He has bestowed on us His precious and exceedingly great promises, so that through them you may escape [by flight] from the moral decay (rottenness and corruption) that is in the world because of covetousness (lust and greed), and become sharers (partakers) of the divine nature (2 Peter 1:4 AMP).

With His divine power flowing through us, we now have the ability to rise above the corruption in the world, which removes our need to hide in shame and guilt. We have become partakers of the divine nature so we can look at ourselves in the mirror and realize He has created us in His image.

> For this very reason, adding your diligence [to the divine promises], employ every effort in exercising your faith to develop virtue

(excellence, resolution, Christian energy), and in [exercising] virtue [develop] knowledge (intelligence), and in [exercising] knowledge [develop] self-control, and in [exercising] self-control [develop] steadfastness (patience, endurance), and in [exercising] steadfastness [develop] godliness (piety), and in [exercising] godliness [develop] brotherly affection, and in [exercising] brotherly affection [develop] Christian love (2 Peter 1:5-7 AMP).

By doing things God's way, we can develop Christian love for others and freely connect with others, not only in the Body of Christ, but we can also draw those who are struggling into right relationship with the Father.

*For as these qualities are yours and increasingly abound in you, **they will keep [you] from being idle or unfruitful** unto the [full personal] knowledge of our Lord Jesus Christ (the Messiah, the Anointed One) (2 Peter 2:8 AMP).*

If our desire is to be fruitful in the Kingdom of God, we will work on these qualities and become progressively more like Him. It is a life-long journey, but great are the rewards!

My Adventure and Journey With God

1. To survive means to: _____

2. To thrive means to: _____

3. Are you surviving or are you thriving? If you are surviving, what do you feel God would have you to do to begin to thrive?

4. In John 10:9-10, why did the Father send Jesus to us?

5. What disconnections do you feel exist in your life and relationships?

6. Read John 10:10 and Ephesians 1:18-23 and embrace the life Christ came to give you. Here is a prayer to pray:

Heavenly Father, I desire to thrive in You and live fully alive in all You have for me. Bring me into the place of thriving in every area of my life. I surrender to Your ways and Your will. Help me understand Your incredible great power that lives in me through Your Son, Jesus Christ. May that power be at work in me all the days of my life. Amen.

BECOMING STRONG TOGETHER

God did choose to heal me. Today I have no lingering effects of the bipolar condition. In walking out this healing journey, I have discovered that God continues to heal things that I didn't even realize were there. God has continued to heal the broken areas of my heart that I had kept hidden. He also continues to renew my mind and transform those areas.

God has continually dealt with any lingering effects of not having my father. Yes, some lingering pain exists in my heart. But the difference is that now I don't have to hide or keep it all inside. I have people around me who I can talk to and who understand the principle of transformation. They encourage me to go to God, talk to Him about what I am going through, and see what He says about it. It's so freeing to be allowed to talk these things through and not feel condemned or criticized but to be encouraged and edified.

For me, that's what the Body of Christ is supposed to be like. We're not to hide our problems and only show our strength. We are to show our weakness and become strong together. Christ said that He didn't come for those who thought they were healthy and strong; He came for the weak and sick.

> Those who are strong and well (healthy) have no need of a physician, but those who are weak and sick. Go and learn what this means: I desire mercy [that is, readiness to help those in trouble] and not sacrifice and sacrificial victims. For I came not to call and invite [to repentance] the righteous (those who are upright and in right standing with God), but sinners (the erring ones and all those not free from sin) (Matthew 9:12-13 AMP).

I believe it's time for the Church to realize and admit just how sick we can be in our times of hurt, pain, and weakness. Then we can encourage one another in the reality that we have the Great Physician who not only can heal us, but also wants each of us to become strong and prosperous.

APPENDIX

Copy of letter from Kenneth P. Phillips, M.D.—Alliance Clinical Associates, S.C. (Oct. 5, 2006).

Definitions:

Anxiety Disorders—In medicine it is defined as a painful or apprehensive uneasiness of mind about some impending or anticipated ill fortune. It is an emotional reaction that manifests in various physical symptoms of different degrees of intensity. Person may not know the source of their anxiety, experiencing persistent anxiety for at least a month without any specific phobia or panic attack.[1]

Brief Psychotic Disorder—The main diagnostic criterion is that the patient has at least one of the following symptoms: delusions, hallucinations, markedly disorganized speech and behavior.[2]

Electroconvulsive (Shock) Therapy—ECT is used mainly for major depressive episodes. Unlike antidepressants, ECT works quickly (often within a few days). Before ECT the patient is anesthetized with a barbiturate and a muscle relaxant. Side effects commonly include temporary memory loss, headaches, and muscle aches.[3]

Manic-Depressive Illness (Bipolar Disorder)—It is characterized by recurring periods of mental illness in which episodes of excitement and hyperactivity (mania) either occur alone or alternate with periods of depression; extreme and unpredictable mood swings from highly excited euphoria to the darkest depths of despair and depression. The person's feelings are so intense that they take over completely, and contact with the real world is lost. In the hyperactive phase, they may be unable to judge the consequences of actions, manifested in shopping sprees, self-destructive sexual behavior, unwise business decisions, reckless driving, also alternate laughing and crying, fleeting delusions or hallucinations. In the depression phase they lose interest and pleasure in nearly all activities, may lose or gain a great deal of weight, change sleep patterns, feel worthless and have trouble concentrating.[4]

Mental Health—An ability to cope with life's transitions, traumatic experiences, and losses in a way that allows your personality to remain intact and even contributes to emotional growth. Instead of attempting to repress all conflicts and distress, the mentally healthy person learns to accept them, to understand them, and to cope with his or her reactions to them so that life can go on. They are able to sustain relationships with family and friends and carry out responsibilities at home and at the workplace with some semblance of harmony. Ideas proceed in a rational manner from one to the next, essentially logical and reasonable.[5]

Panic Attack—An unexplained and unprovoked fight-or-flight response, where body displays the normal physiological response to a life-threatening situation but there is no apparent stimulus: panting, heart pounding, head swimming and palms are damp. Many victims live in a constant state of fear.[6]

Psychiatrist—a medical doctor (M.D.) who completed a four-year course of study in a recognized medical school and four years of post-graduate training (residency) in the specialty of psychiatry. Most are certified by the American Board of Psychiatry and Neurology. Because they are physicians and trained in the use of drugs, they may use medications and write prescriptions.[7]

Psychoanalyst—A psychiatrist or psychologist who has special training in psychotherapy. They will conduct a mental status examination to test thinking patterns, orientation, level of awareness, thought, attention, and judgment.[8]

Psychologist—A person trained in the specialized area of dealing with emotional issues. Most have an advanced degree (Ph.D.) and additional clinical internship training in dealing with patients. They perform psychometric evaluations, use psychotherapy, and sometimes carry out biofeedback relaxation techniques. They do not prescribe medications or do physical examinations.[9]

Psychotherapy—Often used in conjunction with medication to help the depressed person understand the sources of his or her depression and find ways of coping with inner conflicts.[10]

Rapid Cycling—Two or more complete cycles (a manic episode and a major depression that follow each other with no period of remission) occurring within a year.[11]

Seasonal Affective Disorder—*SAD*—An extreme form of "winter blahs" where a person sleeps a great deal in the winter, gains a great deal of weight, is low on energy, highly irritable, headaches, very stressed, and has crying spells.[12]

ENDNOTES

Chapter 1

1. "Depersonalization Disorder," PsychNet-UK, Mental Health and Psychology Directory (accessed Nov. 11, 2009), http://www.psychnet-uk.com/dsm_iv/depersonalization_disorder.htm.

2. Interview of Barbara Findeisen, M.F.C.C., Director of the Star Foundation, a non-profit foundation noted for its research on prenatal and perinatal trauma and the origins and cure of psychological problems by Michael Mendizza, "Lifelong Patterns: Fear or Wholeness" (accessed Nov. 11, 2009), http://www.birthpsychology.com/lifebefore/early.html.

3. En.wikipedia.org/wiki/major depressive disorder.

4. http://www.psychnet-uk.com/dsm_iv/brief_psychotic_episode.htm.

Chapter 2

1. David Chamberlain, Ph.D., "Early Parenting Is Prenatal Parenting," http://www.birthpsychology.com/lifebefore/early.html.

2. Pastor Paulette Horvath, "I have been trained in Theophostic ministry and in the Christian emotional healing method of Elijah House by John and Paul Sandford." Material used with permission.

3. Bruce H. Lipton, Ph.D., "Early and Very Early Parenting, Maternal Emotions and Human Development," (1995), http://www.birthpsychology.com/lifebefore/early.8html.

4. Judith Anne Hahn Terrana, sister of Chrystal's biological father, Carl. Used with permission.

5. Barbara Findeisen, M.F.C.C., Director of the Star Foundation, a nonprofit foundation noted for its research on prenatal and perinatal trauma and the origins and cure of psychological problems, http://www.birthpsychology.com/lifebefore/early.6html.

Chapter 3

1. Judith Anne Hahn Terrana, sister of Chrystal's biological father, Carl. Used with permission.

2. Debbie Hess, Chrystal's best friend from high school. Used with permission.

Chapter 4

1. Used with permission.

2. Chrystal's sister—used with permission.

3. Twila Paris, "The Warrior Is a Child."

Chapter 5

1. Ken Hansen—used with permission.

2. Chuck and Diane Dobbins—used with permission.

3. Ken Hansen—used with permission.

Chapter 6

1. Ken Hansen—used with permission.

2. Used with permission.

3. Monica D. Guillory—used with permission.

4. Used with Ryan's permission.

5. Used with Reneé's permission.

6. Used with Eric's permission.

7. Marla is a close friend of the Hansens from LWCC. Used with permission.

8. Kathy Brothers, Chrystal's college roommate and long-time friend. Used with permission.

Chapter 7

1. AN01057 © 1998-2009 Mayo Foundation for Medical Education and Research (MFMER). All rights reserved. A single copy of these materials may be reprinted for noncommercial personal use only. "Mayo," "Mayo Clinic," "MayoClinic.com," "Embody Health," "Reliable Tools for Healthier Lives," "Enhance Your Life," and the triple-shield Mayo Clinic logo are trademarks of Mayo Foundation for Medical Education and Research.

2. En.wikipedia.org/wiki/major depressive disorder.

3. See letter in the Appendix—Alliance Clinical Associates, S.C., Kenneth P. Phillips, M.D. dated October 2006.

4. Trudy Walk. Taken from session notes. Used with permission.

5. Taken from counseling session notes. Used with permission.

6. Cathy Martin—used with permission.

7. D.J. Nutt, "Relationship of Neurotransmitters to the Symptoms of Major Depressive Disorder," *Journal of Clinical Psychiatry* 69 Suppl E1 (2008): 4-7. PMID 18494537.

8. Used with permission.

9. Stacey Brown—used with permission.

10. Linda Cieseilczyk—used with permission

11. Stacey Brown—used with permission.

12. Debbie and Jim Peters, long-time friends. Ken's best friend. Used with permission.

13. http://www.psychnet-uk.com/dsm_iv/brief_psychotic_episode.htm.

14. Trudy Walk, notes on counseling session. Used with permission.

15. Scott AIF (ed.) et al. (2005). *The ECT Handbook Second Edition: The Third Report of the Royal College of Psychiatrists' Special Committee on ECT* (pdf). Royal College of Psychiatrists, http://www.rcpsych.ac.uk/files/pdfversion/cr128.pdf. Retrieved on July 26, 2008.

16. Ibid.

17. Marla Stob, friend from LWCC—used with permission.

Chapter 8

1. Stacey Brown, Community Life Pastor, Living Water Community Church. Used with permission.

2. Maureen Shafer, Personal Administrative Assistant. Used with permission.

3. Trudy Walk, session notes—used with permission.

4. Used with permission.

5. See documentation in the Appendix section of this book.

6. Marla Stobb—used with permission.

7. Kathy Brothers, Chrystal's college roommate and long-time friend. Used with permission.

8. Marla Stobb—used with permission.

9. Linda Cieseilczyk—used with permission.

Chapter 9

1. Pastor Paulette Horvath—used with permission.

2. Rob Bell, Author of "Sex God."

Chapter 10

1. David P. Armentrout, "Heart Cry: A Biblical Model of Depression," *Journal of Psychology and Christianity* 14, no. 2 (1995), pp. 101-111.

2. Excerpt from David P. Armentrout, "Heart Cry: A Biblical Model of Depression," *Journal of Psychology and Christianity* 14, no. 2 (1995), pages 101-111.

3. Ibid.

4. Pastor Paulette Horvath—used with permission.

5. Armentrout, pp.101-111.

6. http//www.mayoclinc.com/health/depression/DSO175.

7. Paul Sanford, from his Elijah House Basic 1 materials.

8. Denise Baran—used with permission.

9. Testimony used with permission but confidentiality requested.

Chapter 11

1. Ellen Johnson—used with permission.

2. A Greek word for *time*, meaning a moment in time where great change can occur.

3. Meredith Bromfield—used with permission.

4. Cathy Martin—used with permission.

5. Ellen Johnson—used with permission.

6. Patrick—used with permission, confidentiality requested.

7. Ellen Johnson—used with permission.

8. Poem on a greeting card. Author unknown.

Appendix

1. Mayo Clinic: Family Health Book, Anxiety Disorders, © 1993 IVI Publishing Inc.

2. http://www.psychnet-uk.com/dsm_iv/brief_psychotic_ episode.htm.

3. Ibid.

4. Ibid.

5. Mayo Clinic: Family Health Book, *What is Mental Health?* © 1993 IVI Publishing Inc.

6. Ibid.

7. Ibid.

8. Ibid.

9. Ibid.

10. Mayo Clinic: Family Health Book, *Depression and Mood Disorders,* © 1993 IVI Publishing Inc.

11. Ibid.

12. Ibid.

Author's Ministry Page

For more information about Chrystal Hansen, please visit:
www.chrystalhansen.com.

Emerging Life Solutions
C/O Living Water Community Church
190 Lily Cache Lane
Bolingbrook, IL 60440
630-759-5799

Additional copies of this book and other
book titles from DESTINY IMAGE are
available at your local bookstore.

Call toll-free: 1-800-722-6774.

Send a request for a catalog to:

Destiny Image® Publishers, Inc.

P.O. Box 310
Shippensburg, PA 17257-0310

*"Speaking to the Purposes of God for This
Generation and for the Generations to Come."*

**For a complete list of our titles,
visit us at www.destinyimage.com.**